True Self

True Self

Notes on the Essence of Being

Garret Kramer

This book is intended as a reference volume only. It is sold with the understanding that the publisher and author are not engaged in rendering any professional services. The information given here is designed to help you make informed decisions. If you suspect that you have a problem that might require professional treatment or advice, you should seek competent help.

Published by Greenleaf Book Group Press
Austin, Texas
www.gbgpress.com

Distributed by Greenleaf Book Group

For ordering information or special discounts for bulk purchases, please contact Greenleaf Book Group at PO Box 91869, Austin, TX 78709, 512.891.6100.

Design and composition by Greenleaf Book Group
Cover design by Rodrigo Corral

Publisher's Cataloging-in-Publication data is available.

Print ISBN: 978-1-62634-777-9

eBook ISBN: 978-1-62634-778-6

Part of the Tree Neutral® program, which offsets the number of trees consumed in the production and printing of this book by taking proactive steps, such as planting trees in direct proportion to the number of trees used: www.treeneutral.com

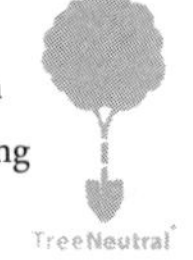

Printed in the United States of America on acid-free paper

23 24 25 26 27 28 29 10 9 8 7 6 5 4 3 2 1

First Edition

For my children, future grandchildren, and all children. May the essence of Being, the knowing of who you truly are—peace, love, and happiness—remain your priority, always.

CONTENTS

FROM THE AUTHOR

True Self is somewhat of a swan song for me. At age fifty-nine, I've decided to close the doors of my consulting company, Inner Sports. It no longer seems logical to coach or serve as a consultant to performers, what I now teach plays poorly on the motivational-speaking circuit, and I'm not interested in worldly pursuits for the sake of fulfillment. In short, self-exploration, and its promise for peace, has become my main focus.

To be clear, as you'll find in this book, self-exploration is not a selfish or even personal focus. Self-exploration is the pathless journey inward. The process of breaking down belief after belief until we arrive at what can't be broken down. The discovery of who we truly are.

I do, however, have one personal concession to make. This book is my legacy, an attempt to provide my children and future grandchildren a glimpse into my life of teaching, consulting, speaking, and writing. *True Self* represents all I hold dear. In the following pages, I resolutely assert that our sole purpose is the knowing of our own Being. For as opposed to any materialistic accomplishment, this knowing is my only wish for the members of my family. And my only wish for you.

A quick word on the book's format: It's presented as a progression of "notes," each ranging between fifty and one thousand words. In section 1, these notes are intended to have you question your conditioned beliefs, particularly the primary belief that the true Self equals a body and mind. In section 2, they go straight to the essence of the true Self. And then, in section 3, they reveal the potential implications of the true Self in the world today. Plus, at the end of each section there are related inquiries and answers meant to summarize what you've read in a more concrete way. These interactions were adapted from both my public talks and the communications I engage in daily. Finally, the book closes with a series of brief reflections. Feel free to use them, share them, whatever you'd like.

One last thing: Self-exploration starts out challenging and gets easier as you go. So if you're initially uncomfortable, unsure, or think that you're a slow study reading *True Self*, stay with it. Our beliefs tend to be stubborn. They tempt us into distraction, coping, or quitting. But that's just ego hanging on for dear life.

Thank you for sharing with me the profound calling that is self-exploration. My appreciation cannot be put into words. And I have neither taken, nor will take, this sacred duty lightly.

Garret Kramer
Morristown, New Jersey, April 2021

Your own self-realization is the greatest service you can render the world.

—Ramana Maharshi

INTRODUCTION

You're about to confront the steady and somewhat ethereal inkling that you've had in the back of your mind since childhood. The one you tried and tried to push away. The one that's been labeled "weird," "eccentric," or "out there." The one you were afraid to discuss with your parents, friends, or even your spouse.

Yes. *That* inkling. The one that had you wondering who you are and what life is all about.

And, yes, that inkling will not let go. Until, that is, you explore it fully. Until you acknowledge that who you are—the true Self—is so much more than you've been led to believe.

So let's acknowledge it:

Who are you?

Please understand, there's not a multiplicity of answers to this, the most fundamental of questions. There are only two options. Two possible perspectives from which the entirety of experience is viewed. And if you're game, I strongly encourage you to make your sole purpose in reading this book an exploration to confirm which perspective is true.

Are you game? Are you ready to courageously explore? To forsake a life of labels, insecurities, and beliefs?

Wonderful. Your initial "step" inward is to pause your reading, and, from where you are right now, simply take note of your experience. See the objects, hear the sounds, smell the smells, feel the ground, breathe the air.

Now consider these two questions:

- Is reality outside of you? Are you a body or object among other objects? Are you experiencing reality from inside a body looking out?

Or . . .

- Is reality within you? Are you seeing, or sensing, from the perspective of the limitless space in which all objects appear, from the perspective of the whole? Are you experiencing the inside of yourself, a world within yourself?

Which is accurate? Can't be both. There can't be two realities.

Obviously, the former is the commonly held view. Forever, it's been accepted that all objects exist separately. It's been taken for granted that we experience from the perspective of a body.

But perhaps it's time we reevaluate this commonly held view.

This book is an invitation to do just that. It's an offer to explore the possibility that because no object can be experienced separate from or outside of the whole, it stands to reason that objects are not only appearances within the whole, they're made of the whole too. For starters, let's call the whole—this limitless space—*Consciousness*. The premise here is that just as whirlpools in the sea are made of the sea, all objects are simply modulations of Consciousness. People, places, things, and even the air are composed of the very same essence with no separation between them.

What's more, as this book will emphasize, a body (a person, a human being) is not a separate object or entity to begin with. Meaning, a body is not the one who experiences (weird, I know). Who you truly are—the one who sees, the one who senses—is perpetually looking within itself at objects made of nothing other than itself.

Once again, take note of your experience.

Whatever you see, hear, smell, taste, or sense, is it made of you? Is it known by you? Does it appear within you?

Who are you?

As I said, you're about to confront the steady inkling that you've had in the back of your mind since childhood.

In this book, I intend to make the case that the knowing of your own Being, knowing who you truly are, is vital for satisfying that steady inkling and curiosity in the back of your mind. But equally vital, this knowing is the virtually undisclosed prerequisite for constructive change, for moral behavior, and for world peace.

- Why, for example, do you suppose that we can't live in harmony?
- Why, in spite of protests, activism, and forward-thinking laws, do poverty, discrimination, and war still occur?

- What's the actual root of pollution and environmental degradation? Of addiction, stress, and worry?
- Why have research, science, and psychology struggled to produce long-term results?
- Why does life seem an endless cycle of pleasure and pain?

Now I realize that's quite a few questions and so-called "problems" right out of the gate. Yet what if I told you that the answers to these questions and the solutions to these problems—to essentially all problems—start in the exact same place?

What if this starting point is right under our noses, hiding in plain sight?

What if this starting point is merely our culture's conditioning, the commonly held view that I mentioned earlier?

What if this conditioning (programming, indoctrination) has shrouded our true nature, convinced us that the appearance of separation, division, and distinct objects is genuine, when it's been an illusion the entire time?

I'm not blaming our culture. Admittedly, my work has played a part in supporting this illusion. As a teacher, consultant, speaker, and author, my job (or so I thought) was to help bring out the best in others. To be the expert. To know. And although, to be frank, I labored to find this knowing while catering to the illusion of separation, I did become what many would label "successful." I worked with some of the finest athletes, coaches, teams, organizations, and performers in the world. They won.

They achieved. To a certain extent, they found contentment off the field of play.

My primary message?

Prior to writing this book, my message, which fills the pages of my previous books, *Stillpower* and *The Path of No Resistance*, was twofold:

- Circumstances have no influence over you.
- Any mental strategy, tool, technique, or ritual implemented for the purpose of making you feel and perform better does not work.

And today, I pretty much stand by this two-part message. But it wasn't until about six years ago when I had the following heart-to-heart chat with a client, a National Hockey League player, that I recognized the true basis of this message and how it was actually guiding those with whom I had worked.

Here, as far as I remember, is what happened:

At the close of a morning meeting in my office, this hockey player spontaneously said, "G, what I love about our time together is that you always point me back to my true Self."

Trying to conceal my bewilderment, I replied, "And how would you define the true Self?"

"Hmm," he murmured. "It's a feeling I can't put into words. But I suppose what you've taught me is that there's more to life than meets the eye. It's like there's this one version of me, a version that's hurt by things and needs to fend off those things with coping tools and techniques. A version I'm not sure is true. But then there's another version, the version you keep reminding me of, which is innately resilient, always whole, and one with everything and everyone. The true Self."

To be fair, I wasn't sure that I had spoken with him about any of that. And I had definitely never referenced the true Self. But the first thing that occurred to me (and I didn't share this with anyone for weeks) was:

This is it!

For what seemed like my entire life, including my working life, I knew I was close. I knew I was on the cusp of seeing who I am, and who we are. But in the thirty seconds it took for me to hear—deeply hear—his words, I knew that my world would never be the same.

My client may not have grasped the magnitude of what he had said. But with the feeling behind his words, he had directed me straight to the essence of my own Being. He had turned me around. I was staring directly at Source, the true Self, Consciousness, God.

I was home.

You and I are about to embark on a similar journey back home to who we are. To Source. To the essence of Being. The "notes" in this book detail what I now teach and where I point audiences, performers, organizations, coaches, and other teachers. These notes are also filled with examples of the implications of this teaching. And while at this stage, an idea such as "the essence of Being" likely seems strange, by the end of the book you will:

1. Know who you are not—a separate self.
2. Know who, or what, you are—the true Self, Consciousness. Other often-used terms: *Source*, *God*, *God's infinite Being*, *Awareness*, *I am*, as well as *peace*, *love*, and *happiness*. (In this book, *the universe* too.)
3. Be in the world from this newly uncovered perspective.

But not just yet. Before we leave the Introduction, let's jump back to the culturally conditioned belief in separation. Indeed, this unproven belief—also known in some circles as *duality* and in others as *materialism**—which proposes that a subject (the knower) and objects (the things known by the subject) exist separate from one another, is the foundation of every misfortune or problem ever known.

Is this a bold statement?

From where I sit, no. And my aim is for you to sit here too. So, as *one*, we can do our part to finally shift an innocent-but-blind world inward.

In other words, just as my client did for me, and just as I've been doing ever since, my aim is to point you away from the material world—or, as it's also called, the *object-based world*—and inward toward the true Self, the complete opposite direction from where you've been conditioned to look. Then off you'll go, living from your newfound understanding and becoming a beacon of it.

*The definition of *materialism* as I use it is a precursor of this more common definition: "The tendency to consider material possessions and physical comfort as more important than spiritual values."

Now I'm not saying it will be easy. As you'll see, the ego—the product of the primary belief that "I am a separate self"—will strongly kick back. But this book is designed to help you keep moving. Not outward toward objects (substances, activities, accolades, relationships, states of mind, etc.). Not toward gaining information, resisting what is, or seeking something better. But inward toward the dissolution of all that is *not* essential.

For only a turning away from the object-based world can bring what is essential, that which you have always longed for.

Why?

Because when we turn away from the lure of seeking relief in objects, automatically and without effort we turn inward toward peace, love, and happiness.

And while, again, this turn inward will bring discomfort to who you are not—since ultimately it will dismantle the illusion of ego—rest assured, who you are will not be harmed.

So are you ready to courageously explore?

Very good.

Let's turn away from objects and turn toward Consciousness.

Toward Source.

Toward the Being we share.

Toward the singular, or non-dual, essence of all things.

Toward your greatest possible gift to the universe, and what this book is about, knowing your Self, *truly*.

1.

The Dissolution of Belief

Let's begin slowly, sort of, with these questions:

Is there any doubt that thoughts happen within you? Is there any doubt that it's you who experiences a world? No and no, of course. But here's the rub:

Has a thought ever been located inside a body?

Not as of yet.

Have the means or pathways through which a body experiences a world ever been found?

Not as of yet.

Hence, this book.

Rather than analyze thoughts, rather than search for the personal power to experience, rather than adhere to the belief that thoughts happen within a body or that a body is aware, rather than follow belief after belief after belief—all of which stem from the primary belief that "who you are *is* a body" and that "who you are shares the limits and destiny of a body"—I ask merely this:

Hold still and explore this self that you've been conditioned to assume yourself to be.

Who is the "I" in which thoughts appear?

Who is the "I" who has experiences or is aware?

The first step on our inward journey is this, the fundamental question:

Who am I?

Without the answer to this question, without the realization that this "I" is not the body, not a person, not a separate self, your foundation will be one of belief. Yet peace, love, and happiness—the true Self—are found in the absence of belief.

WHAT IF?

Rather than from the perspective of a distinct person who experiences all things outside of yourself, imagine that you are the infinite and eternal universe and that all things arise and fall inside of you.

Imagine that all things are one with you.

Imagine that there's no outside of you at all.

Now imagine that this perspective was known far and wide to be true.

What would be different about the world?

What would the implications be for the world?

What would the implications be for *you*?

SELF-EXPLORATION

Also known as self-realization, self-inquiry, self-discovery, or self-reflection—what is *self-exploration*?

For our purposes, it's simply the process of exploring the

accumulated beliefs that you've accepted as true, despite having no direct experience of their validity.

From exploring run-of-the-mill beliefs ("positive thoughts, positive results") to exploring deeply ingrained beliefs ("I was born and will die"), this process prevents the reliance on objects and others.

Self-exploration is the pathless path to Source.

The pathless path home.

Home is where you're now heading.

THE ROOT OF YOUR TROUBLES

It's a pretty fair bet that until now, you've made the following assumption:

A body is conscious, or aware.

Even the standard definition of Consciousness—the state of being aware of one's surroundings; the awareness or perception of something by a person—is based on this assumption.

But the thing is, you have no evidence that a body, or what you call *your* body, is more aware than the chair you sit in right now.

And this misunderstanding is at the root of all of your troubles.

And dispelling this misunderstanding is the reason I wrote this book.

IT BEGINS WITH CONDITIONING

So where does this misunderstanding—the shrouding of the true Self, the belief that "I am an aware body or person," the notion that "I am limited and lacking," the theory that objects are truly separate and distinct—begin?

Look no further than today's culture of "follow the leader," the conditioning that has us listening to and believing experts.

An expert says:

- "Find your why." And seeking in a world of objects has begun.
- "It's better to be this kind of person." And discrimination has begun.
- "You control your thoughts, attitudes, and actions." And self-blame has begun.
- "A cluttered mind is unproductive." And coping mechanisms have begun.
- "We stand for these core values." And brainwashing has begun.
- "America is number one." And arrogance has begun.
- "Effort is essential." And tension has begun.
- "Connect with others." And separation has begun.
- "Laud the military." And indoctrination has begun.
- "Trust the data, the science." And the veiling of intuition has begun.
- "Beware of external enemies." And paranoia has begun.

- "Every failure is a chance for success." And rationalization has begun.
- "Time is precious." And desperation has begun.
- "Worship God." And religion has begun.
- "It's about being human." And suffering has begun.

So many experts. So many messages. So many viewpoints. Which to believe? Which to follow?

The answers are none and none.

The popularity of an expert, message, or viewpoint is a smoke screen, a decoy.

Truth, at the end of the day, stands the test of your own experience. At the end of the day, follow just that.

THE BENEFIT OF INSECURITY

While experts, our entire culture it seems, have also conditioned you to try to fix insecurity, your attempts to fix it have you resisting the most beneficial intuitive sign.

Insecurity means that you're looking outward for answers. You're trying to connect your identity to, or find your well-being in, relationships, rewards, and status.

That is, if and when insecurity appears—it's supposed to!

Insecurity is a reminder to not seek further in the material world. To not try to cope (or pursue relief). To not do battle with your current experience.

Insecurity is a welcomed sign to turn inward.

AVOIDING TRUTH

Beliefs are invented to rid yourself of insecurity, or of any feeling.

But the idea that you can rid yourself of a feeling is itself a belief. A mistruth. Where would a feeling go? That's why seeking to relieve a feeling keeps you in the realm of belief, in the grip of that feeling, and ultimately away from truth.

Have you stacked so many beliefs upon yourself that you no longer know yourself? That you no longer know what's true?

It's OK.

Let's explore your beliefs.

You've been innocently avoiding truth.

Until now.

WHICH IS TRUE?

In order for an object in the world (a person, thought, theory, strategy, technique, or word of wisdom) to be of service to you (perhaps by easing suffering, connecting you with others, instilling inspiration, or providing freedom), you yourself would have to be an object in the world.

Are you an object in the world?

Or . . .

Are the world and all objects within you?

Are you a speck in the universe?

Or . . .

Are you the universe?

A speck is made of the universe.

But is the universe made of a speck?

There's either duality or there's not duality.

Either you're an object in the world, or the world and all objects are within you.

Explore direct experience.

Which is actually true?

NO IDEA

Today, to seemingly help you thrive as an object in the world, you can easily find:

- Fitness advice
- Relationship advice
- Nutrition advice
- Business advice
- How-to-be-more-confident advice
- How-to-end-addiction advice
- Love-your-neighbor advice
- Find-your-life-purpose advice
- How-to-play-better advice
- How-to-feel-better advice
- How-to-lead-better advice
- Money advice
- Political advice

- How-to-save-the-world advice
- How-to-be-more-creative advice
- Mental health advice

And you have no idea who the heck you are.

HAS IT HAPPENED?

It may not have happened, yet. But at some point, you'll question whether happiness can be found in the content of experience. Can objects (substances, activities, accolades, relationships, and states of mind) truly bring the fulfillment you seek?

Not only that, but at some point, distracting yourself away from unhappiness will no longer make sense. Objects sought for the purpose of finding happiness will be revealed as the waste of energy they are. You'll realize that these mechanisms are merely layers upon layers, further shrouding happiness and fulfillment.

For most people, rather unfortunately, this realization occurs extremely late in life. It's revealing, for instance, that those close to death don't yearn for more possessions. For them, the realization *has* set in. They frequently regret the lifelong chase for happiness and fulfillment through the acquisition of objects. It's obvious that answers can't be found in the object-based (or material) world.

Now if you're pondering where answers—happiness and fulfillment—can be found, fair enough. But this book will not start up that same materialistic search once more.

Simply consider this:

Cease connecting, or trying to connect, your well-being to objects. Cease connecting your resilience to anything that changes, appears and disappears, or comes and goes. Cease connecting your security to anything that, by nature, is insecure. Cease connecting *who you are* to *who you are not.*

And then?

What remains will be none other than you. Exactly where happiness and fulfillment are found. As you're perhaps beginning to take note, there's never a path from you, the true Self, to you.

EXPERIENCE AND REALITY

A key element of my work is reminding people of the futility of trying to fix, control, or alter their experiences. If you didn't know much about my work prior to picking up this book (if you hadn't been introduced to the fact that objects of experience can't bring happiness and fulfillment), this element will probably surprise you. You might wonder why, if you're having a bad or anxious experience, your best option is to not try to fix it.

Short answer: Experience is not what it seems to be.

To demonstrate, let's say you're an ice hockey player and you're in the midst of a troubling experience. Your coach doesn't care about you; he's treating you poorly. You're getting angry and frustrated. You want relief from your troubles, which you think your coach is causing.

But what if your troubles aren't caused by your coach? What

if your troubles are triggered by the culturally conditioned belief that you, a "subject," and the objects of your experience exist separate from one another (as presented in the Introduction: duality, materialism)? What if all troubles are brought about by the misunderstanding that objects take place separate from or outside of you? After all, take away *you* and does your coach even exist? If the answer is yes, how do you know that for sure? If the answer is no, then your coach can't be the cause of anything, your troubles included. (If this seems unclear, hang in there. Much of this book will illuminate this very point.)

It's mind-bending at times to think about, but experiences are always arising and dissolving within. Sure, you can immerse yourself in experiences. You can passionately take part. You can play the game of life, and of hockey, freely. It's just essential to first consider whether the content of experience (objects) that seem separate from you, truly are.

No you, no experiences.

That's why trying to fix or fight your experiences is futile—not to mention extremely taxing and potentially destructive.

Let's continue to explore.

THE IRRESPONSIBLE THEORY OF PERSONAL RESPONSIBILITY

I'm about to make a claim with which you'll likely take umbrage.

How do I know?

Because I've made the same claim to nearly every person, group, or audience I've spoken to. And each has reacted with disbelief—at first.

Here's the claim:

> *There's no such thing as personal responsibility. No person possesses the power to control or manage thoughts, choices, or behaviors.*

Taking umbrage?

I get it. But reflect on these questions:

Do you control the millions of processes taking place within you right now? Do you control moods? Do you control reflexes? Do you control digestion? Do you control whether you cry at the movies?

Why, then, do you assume that you're responsible for certain other processes, behaviors, or choices? Is it conceivable that while you don't control 99 percent of what takes place within you, that you're somehow responsible for 1 percent?

I actually don't blame you. In my work, I sometimes make allowances for this common assumption. Besides, in self-help circles today, a familiar mantra is "control what you can control," with attitude, effort, positivity, and body language being among the so-called "controllables."

But see if your experience lines up.

Maybe those who buy into the notion that they're responsible for their actions are the ones most bound up, sullen, and burdened? Maybe they're the ones whose behavior is most out of control? Could it be that it's in trying to exercise personal responsibility or control over what can't be controlled that tension reigns and peace is sequestered?

Look at the disharmony of the world. Most people believe

in and try to take on personal responsibility. As we're observing more and more each day, however, perhaps this belief is due for a complete reexamination.

CONTROLLING MYSELF

On the topic of control, here's one aspect that I'm guessing you'd say is obvious:

> *You don't possess the power to control if and when a thought occurs.*

In my experience, this aspect or understanding is indeed obvious to most. But, interestingly, so is the following misunderstanding:

> *You do possess the power to control what you do with a thought once it occurs.*

Let's clear this up straightaway.

A thought occurs out of your control. Then the choice of whether to manage, change, follow, or not follow that thought—which is nothing more than another thought—also occurs out of your control.

For example:

> *I want to tell that dude off* = *a thought*

> *No, I'm not going to tell that dude off* = *another thought*

All choices present themselves in the form of a thought. And, as we discussed, you're not responsible for, and don't possess the power to control, any thought that occurs.

WHERE IS THIS POWER?

The next time a guru insists that you do own the personal power to choose (and they will), gently inquire:

"Where in me is this power?"

If "In the mind" is the answer, ask, "Where in the mind?"

If "In the brain" is the answer, ask, "Where in the brain?"

If "In this cortex" is the answer, ask, "Where in this cortex?" . . . and so on.

Eventually, the guru will realize that he or she has no idea where to find the power "to choose."

Because the power to choose is found in one place: belief.

FREE WILL AND PREDESTINATION ARE NOT OPPOSITES

A quick and possibly challenging note on another common belief regarding choice and control: the belief that free will and predestination are opposites. Not to mention the belief that they're the only two options.

They are not.

Free will and predestination are both implications of the primary belief that "I am a separate self." They're implications of the belief, or misunderstanding, that the separation we perceive is real. Absent of this belief, separate occurrences in time—whether chosen through free will or predestined by God—could not exist.

Absent of the belief in separation, time is but a concept.

There is *here*, there is *now*. There is you.

FREE WILL: CONCEPT AND TRUTH

We've landed at this intriguing question, one often debated in spiritual, and not so spiritual, communities:

Is there such a thing as free will?

Yes, there is.

But free will, like time, is only a concept. A functional or practical idea. For people to legitimately possess free will, for free will to be true and not a concept, separate people and the objects they're free to choose must be more than just appearances (images, modulations, or vibrations) within the whole. People and objects must be independent entities.

As we'll address head-on throughout section 1:

- Are you a separate, independent person?
- Are there separate, independent objects from which to choose?
- How could anything exist separate from or independent of that which is whole?
- How could anything exist on its own?

Resolve those questions. Then let me know whether, above and beyond a concept, free will is true.

THE RELAXATION OF EFFORT

Let's now move to the topic of *effort*, yet another familiar concept. The concept that busting our butts is necessary to get somewhere in the world. As with free will, this concept is neither good nor bad. No concept is. It would be a mistake, though, to accept effort as a necessity when there's nothing absolutely necessary about it.

Effort, as I define it, involves having to work against a separate and conflicting force in order to get somewhere or achieve something. This force could be an apparent roadblock, a circumstance you disagree with, or even your own thoughts and feelings. As such, effort is but another offshoot of the belief in separation—of duality, materialism—the mistruth that two or more things exist as separate entities.

Say, for example, I'm preparing to go for a run. I'm tying my running shoes when it occurs to me to stay home and relax. Now there's a potential for conflict and effort, as I suddenly feel the stress of needing to push through my conflict, make the right choice, and be my most productive self.

But should I push or exert effort in this way?

To find the answer, let's examine whether the two "separate" and conflicting forces (thoughts in this case) are indeed separate.

Where do they arise?

Within me.

What are they made of?

Me.

So freely take your pick. One thought is no different and can't be more "right" than the other. (When this happens, I tend to stick with my initial plan.)

The bottom line on effort is that the impulse to exert it is merely an indication that you're falling for the conditioning around effort that's been thrust upon you since forever: the belief that it's necessary. You've overlooked the singular, or non-dual, essence of the whole. You've mistaken your thoughts (*go for a run*, *stay home and relax*) for separate, conflicting entities. You're busting your butt to make the right choice when there is no right choice. All "choices" are equivalent. They're made of the same stuff.

As you'll find moving forward in this book, the impulse to exert effort shouldn't be taken to heart because the appearance of separation shouldn't be taken to heart. Effort—as well as conflict—takes place on behalf of a separate self. The true Self, by contrast, equals the relaxation of effort.

IT SEEMS TO YOU

- It seems to you that saving the earth is important, so you push saving the earth on others.
- It seems to you that positivity is important, so you push positivity on others.
- It seems to you that working hard is important, so you push working hard on others.
- It seems to you that a certain diet is important, so you push a certain diet on others.
- It seems to you that love of country is important, so you push love of country on others.

- It seems to you that vaccination is important, so you push vaccination on others.
- It seems to you that seeking success is important, so you push seeking success on others.
- It seems to you that capitalism is important, so you push capitalism on others.
- It seems to you that resisting a political position is important, so you push resistance on others.

How's it working out?

Perhaps harmony can't be found by pushing, or even sharing, your personal and programmed opinions.

And, yes, that's an opinion too.

Back to exploring the nature of who we are.

THE CONFOUNDING ASPECT OF BELIEF

Imagine this scenario:

A person named Garret is suffering. You might say he's depressed. Because our culture believes that suffering is a sign of dysfunction (belief #1 in this scenario), that suffering has to be fixed (belief #2), and that certain people can be trained to help other people fix suffering (belief #3), Garret then seeks the counsel of one of these trained people, an expert. First step? The expert attempts to figure out why Garret is suffering—there has to be a why (belief #4). The expert then goes through a checklist of possible reasons (each reason itself representing another belief).

Garret is suffering because . . .

a. Of his past

b. Of his conditioning

c. Of his biology

d. Of his circumstances

e. Of his thinking

f. He's not positive or confident

g. He doesn't understand others

h. He doesn't understand his mind and how to control it

i. Etc., etc., etc.

Garret then identifies with one or more of these reasons (belief #5). And he and the expert work through a method or process (belief #6) to help him overcome this diagnosed cause of his suffering.

But let's take a huge step back.

Following the beliefs of our culture is what led Garret to meet with the expert. And now the expert (who, while well-intentioned, is also following cultural beliefs) has presented Garret with potential causes for his struggle that didn't even exist to Garret until this meeting.

In other words, using reason *f* as an example, Garret now believes that he's suffering because he lacks positivity or confidence. Although prior to this meeting, that thought had never crossed his mind!

A belief leading to a belief leading to a belief. A never-ending search outward.

How about this instead?

When presented with someone's perspective on an issue, including that of an expert, ask yourself:

- Is it accurate?
- Does it align with my actual experience?
- Is it a belief?

And as for suffering, we've been following beliefs for long enough. Just because an expert or our culture says that something is true does not make it true. What if, contrary to what we've been told, the beliefs that feelings or sensations like suffering have a cause, require a cure, and indeed can be cured are where prolonged suffering comes from?

I'd say it does come from these beliefs.

But please, don't believe me.

NO CURES, NO SUFFERING

Here's more on the beliefs we've been sold about suffering:

So-called "cures" for suffering—psychological theories and methods, mental strategies and techniques, or understandings of the mind—are what give rise to suffering. Suffering does not give rise to cures.

Meditate on your own experience:

A sensation appears. It isn't, by nature, inherently right or wrong. How could it be? But if you learn about a cure for that sensation—in a workshop, in a book, from a guru or expert—now you have a problematic sensation. A sensation that must be focused on and dealt with. A sensation not as worthy as another. A sensation that was merely a sensation until you were taught otherwise (as Garret was by the expert in the previous note).

Our starting place is different. Self-exploration is initiated from a place of sheer interest and wonder. The remedy of suffering is not the intent.

Without seeking and applying cures, what do you then suppose happens to the sensation of suffering?

DID YOU LEARN THAT?

- Is a particular sensation unbearable, or did you learn that it is?
- Are you a human being, or did you learn that you are?
- Were you born, or did you learn that you were?
- Will you die, or did you learn that you will?
- Do objects appear outside of you, or did you learn that they do?

Belief leading to belief leading to belief. A ton of confusion.

- What didn't you learn?
- What does direct experience reveal?
- What's not a belief?

When you discover what's not a belief, you will have found that which is veiled by beliefs.

You will have found the underlying aim of all seeking.

You will have found yourself.

A MASTER OF DECEIT

Ego, in this book, refers to the veiling of the true Self. The belief that "not only do I experience separate objects but I, too, am a separate object." The belief that "other objects appear outside of me." Ego is the product of the belief that separation is real.

And while the ego can cause no harm—as both separation and the ego are not real—people will still work like the dickens to maintain the ego's imagined existence. This habit pertains to everyone without exception, including those in positions of authority, leadership, or expertise. The belief that "I am a separate object or person" is the most insidious of beliefs. It's the foundation of all other beliefs. It's the toughest belief to shake.

For example, ego will claim that it is: *resilient, wise, loving.* It will suggest that it owns the power to: *think, feel, perceive.* It will insist that you come to it for: *well-being, clarity, growth*. It will validate separateness through zen-sounding theories along the lines of: *separate realities, levels of consciousness, higher states of mind.* It will promote the following delusions as positive: *diversity, agreeing to disagree, the delineation of borders*. It will tout coping methods, distractions, and self-defense strategies such as: *affirmations, sticking to routines, discarding negative people.* It will coax you into these behaviors and attitudes as personal paths to peace: *gratitude, forgiveness, acceptance.* It will aggrandize itself by taking advantage of and selling cures for the culturally conditioned ideas of: *fear, desire, lack.* It will insist that the material world is a place to find: *purpose, contentment, love.* It will twist spiritual words and mantras in order to entrench as real the illusion of separateness: *"good deeds for others bring blessings," "nurture your own soul," "pray to a distant God."* Finally, to stay relevant and necessary, the ego will continually replay the misunderstanding that who you truly are is a separate individual. It will endorse: *self-belief, confidence, personal responsibility.*

Rather than follow the beliefs of one who deems himself or herself to be separate, rather than follow an expert or guru, rather than follow anyone, I again encourage you to check in with your own experience.

Has a separate self, separate object, separate world, separate universe, or separate God ever been found?

What do *you* say?

Can you find any of those separate from or outside of yourself?

Is separation real?

From the perspective of no separation, is there anything to resist, seek, or cope with?

From the perspective of no separation, is there anything to fix? Anyone to hurt, punish, or with whom to settle scores?

From the perspective of no separation, isn't peace guaranteed?

Experience transcends belief. Look to experience, not to the beliefs—the deceit—of the ego.

Look to yourself.

Answers are there.

THE LURE OF EGO

Let's examine more objects of conditioning that the ego exploits to maintain not only its illusory existence but its lure, the guru's lure of "Come to me for all that you seek."

Here's a short list:

- Achieving goals
- Making money
- Choosing better thoughts and feelings

Question:

Have these objects proved satisfying?

I don't mean temporary satisfaction or relief. Have you found permanent satisfaction in them?

No doubt, the ego will implore you to keep seeking in the world of objects. It will convince you to pay (sometimes big bucks) for help in the gathering of objects.

But, instead, let's consider not seeking objects at all. Let's explore what's not an object.

And what might that be?

It's what's permanent. It's the title of this book. You've been seeking it all along. The true Self.

THE SELF CANNOT KNOW GOD

You try so hard, but . . .

A self cannot know *peace.*

A self cannot know *love.*

A self cannot know *happiness.*

A self cannot know *God*.

These are the interchangeable names we give to what's real, names synonymous with Source. And while it's noble to try, the self (the body, the mind, the personal) cannot access its Source, it cannot know the spiritual.

So don't try harder. Inquire:

Is the separate self real?

Are you, the one who experiences separate selves, a separate self?

Our exploration is a calling to stop searching far and wide for peace, love, and happiness. To stop searching for God. To scrutinize direct experience and find out if duality—"*here* is me, and *there* is everything else that is separate from me"—is or is not true.

"Who am I?"

Set aside the belief in separation and you'll see. Peace, love, happiness—and God—are always with you. Perhaps they are you, after all.

YOUR EXPERIENCE

When I talk about direct experience, I'm not referring to what you've learned from a parent, coach, friend, or partner. I'm not referring to the reported perceptions and sensations of any separate self.

I'm talking about your experience prior to conditioning. Only yours. Because without realizing it, you've spent much of your life drifting away from direct experience. You've overlooked what your experience truly means. You've likely lived from the presumption that you are a separate self who lives in a world of separate selves and objects. You've adopted for yourself the labels through which most people describe and evaluate material things. You've bought into the culturally conditioned belief that separation, duality, or materialism is true or real. And while this still may seem relatively insignificant, I promise it is not.

But please, don't take my word for any of this. Check out whether, in *your* experience, the following add up:

- All things appear within the whole.
- All things are one with the whole.
- All things are made of the whole.

Do these ideas seem accurate? Kind of? Here's more:

- Separation is an illusion (all things are made of the same substance).
- You are not a separate self.

Make sense now? Still only kind of? No rush.

Based on your experience, let's break down belief after belief until answers become obvious.

Your experience is and always will be the only true teacher.

EXPLORE THIS, NOT THAT

Explore what the mind is made of. For you cannot find peace of mind if you don't understand what the mind is made of.

Explore what money is made of. For you cannot gain financial security if you don't understand what money is made of.

Explore what the environment is made of. For you cannot save the environment if you don't understand what the environment is made of.

Explore what people are made of. For you cannot end discrimination and conflict if you don't understand what people are made of.

Explore what diseases are made of. For you cannot heal and be well if you don't understand what diseases are made of.

Explore what suffering is made of. For you cannot flourish, as suffering will overwhelm you, if you don't understand what suffering is made of.

You need not explore how any of the preceding work, interact, or function. That will become clear once you grasp the singular essence of all things.

You're reading *True Self* to explore this singular essence. All curiosity is a pull toward this essence, your essence, a pull inward.

Let's stay on the direct and pathless path. The rest will fluidly, and lovingly, take care of itself.

SEEKING FIXES

How about problems? Do you suffer from them? Seek fixes for them?

"Problems," as you'll see, stray us from the direct and pathless path.

Most everyone seems to be dealing with some form of problem these days. A billion-dollar industry—self-help, motivation, coaching, and counseling—even stands primed to help us deal.

But how are we doing?

With the evolution of this industry and its experts, are we more at peace? More loving? Less discriminatory? Is the environment cleaner? Are we more productive? Any less stressed?

You know the answer. Generation after generation, we're consumed by the same problems. We've tried millions of methods. After all this time, is it actually possible that we're going to discover the method, guru, tool, or technique that will help do the trick?

Highly unlikely.

But what if there is no problem-solving method? What if methods are the reason we keep perpetuating our problems? And our suffering? What if *not trying to fix* is the ultimate solution?

Highly likely.

Here's why (and please read slowly):

Problems result from a resistance to what is. No resistance, no problems. No problems, no problems to solve. Consider that there's a baked-in fatal flaw when it comes to problem-solving. It requires the labeling of a situation as both "problematic" and "fixable." And labeling (the attempt to divide a situation or any object from the whole) is the very act of resisting the non-dual essence of the whole, resisting what is. Seeking fixes is the seed of all problems. We cannot fix what is not real. We cannot sever a situation, a problem, from that which is whole.

To end our generational "problem cycle," then, we must do the opposite of what our suffering (not to mention the self-help industry) is asking us to do. We must stop problem-solving. We must stop seeking fixes.

For when seeking fixes comes to an end, suffering dissolves.

And "problems"?

They're seen as nothing other than current situations to experience and take part in, which are made of the whole.

THE INDUSTRY

Let's dig a bit deeper into the self-help industry. It's an industry designed around the suffering brought about by both the conditioned impulse to *resist* "what is" (as I just alluded) and to *seek* a different or finer version of "what is" (as I'll allude in this note, think of resisting and seeking as two sides of the same coin).

And that's not all when it comes to the industry.

Instead of making it clear that seeking breeds suffering, the industry's baseline, its standard, is to "cure" suffering. It does this through coping strategies, defense mechanisms, distractions, techniques, and methods to follow. The industry rightfully knows that the application of cures correlates with rapid relief. (I'll explain why this is in a second.)

But here's the industry's game: It also knows that seeking—and suffering—will ramp up again. It knows that people will then turn to another cure. Then another. Then another.

Why, you might ask, do industry experts keep reinforcing this agonizing cycle? Why don't they reveal that coping strategies, defense mechanisms, distractions, techniques, and methods can't cure a thing? Why don't they point out that relief only occurs upon the interruption of seeking? Why aren't they forthright about the fact that people often interrupt seeking and briefly experience relief *because* they've been convinced by the industry that they now have "the cure"?

The answer is that these experts don't understand it themselves. If they did, they wouldn't offer coping strategies and the like in the first place.

It's not on purpose, mind you. They, too, have been taught to apply cures in their own lives. So they continue to seek, find temporary relief, and then suffer just like the rest.

Perhaps the self-help industry requires an immediate overhaul. The industry promotes seeking. When in the absence of seeking—seeking to escape one's current experience, seeking a new and better experience, or seeking a new and better cure—suffering cannot arise.

THE DIFFERENCE

Typically, when a performer, team, or organization is considering hiring me, I'm asked some variety of the following question:

"With all the self-help experts, motivational gurus, psychologists, and mind coaches to choose from, what's different about your approach?"

My stock answer (which provokes disinterest about 95 percent of the time):

"My approach is self-inquiry. Rather than overlay strategy or methodology upon the personal self we've been conditioned to believe ourselves to be, my approach is the process of questioning the very nature of this self."

In other words, because the belief in a personal or separate self is the foundation of all forms of tension, turmoil, and suffering, to find lasting peace, we must first uproot this belief. We must become utterly certain that we are not the needy, lacking, and isolated product of our conditioning—a personal self. We must come to understand that the power to experience, know, and even think does not reside within a body.

I'm not suggesting, however, that self-inquiry is right for everyone at any given moment. Most of us are wooed by and dependent on the thrills and chills of the material world. Most of us crave comfort. Most of us long to belong. Most of us aim to preserve or enhance the body. So it's perfectly appropriate to exhaust a wide range of materialistic options before we're prepared to eradicate seeking in the material world. Or before we realize that we cannot find who we are by forsaking who we are. Most of us are simply not yet interested in the basic and, dare I say, placid potential of self-inquiry.

But for those called to hold still, for those ready to allow the mind to fold inward, the pathless path is the only game in town.

What's different about self-inquiry? It asks us to turn away from the conditioning that has us trying to satisfy wants and needs, and, instead, take a genuine look at the one who's been conditioned to want and need. Self-inquiry is not personal. It's not self-help. It dissolves the belief that "I am a body" and brings us straight back to Source, to Consciousness, to love, to our singular Being. Self-inquiry places who we truly are front and center.

TO UNDERSTAND

Further inquiry:

Do your thoughts churn outward? Do you seek salvation in the material world? Does this habit lead to resistance, suffering, and separation?

Or . . .

Do your thoughts fold inward?

Thoughts, and deeds, churn outward as a result of *misunderstanding.*

They fold inward as a result of *understanding.*

This is why understanding the essence of ourselves, rather than seeking to comfort ourselves, is our highest and only true calling. The fundamental question—"Who am I?"—delivers us straight back to Source.

If we must seek, then let's (in a manner of speaking) seek the true Self.

Let's travel inward.

Let's find understanding, once more.

ON LOYALTY

A perhaps surprising aspect of the conditioning that has us seeking to satisfy wants and needs in the material world is *loyalty*. As I'm sure you're familiar, we're conditioned to profess personal loyalty to individuals, nationalities, ethnicities, organizations, political parties, value systems, and religions.

Yet not only does this conditioning produce blind followers, servants, and automatons, it also gives credence to the primary conditioned belief that "I am a limited and lacking separate self," the belief that has us seeking in the material world to begin with. Like all misunderstandings, object-based loyalty stalls the divulgence of truth.

Real loyalty is the opposite of servitude.

Free yourself from the old. Free yourself from conditioning.

Turn around, away from seeking to become part of something greater in the material world.

Know the essence of Being. Your essence. Our essence.

Remain loyal to that.

YOU CAN'T TRUST THIS

We often hear of "the necessity of trust," but that is cloaked in the same misunderstanding as loyalty. Nonetheless, it's rampant in the coaching, scientific, and New Age spirituality arenas.

"Team members must trust one another." "Trust the expert/your partner/your friend."

But be honest. You struggle with this type of advice, don't you? Doesn't trying to trust feel forced? Doesn't it constantly let you down?

You're not alone. And here's why:

It's impossible to trust another. You cannot trust or depend on something impermanent—as in any object, including people. What's impermanent, by definition, is untrustworthy.

Do you yearn to trust?

Trust the permanent. The infinite, the eternal. The shared space, or Being, within which all things appear, and out of which they are made.

ENDING CONFLICT

As opposed to trust, do you often find yourself in conflict with others?

Don't like it?

Want to find common ground?

No worries. Simply examine not what you have right, but what you have wrong.

For what you have wrong is the root belief: "I am a separate self that's limited and lacking."

Which is precisely what the so-called "others you're in conflict with" have wrong too.

SILENCING EGO

There's always something new to learn or old to dispel. Case in point: my short take on conflict. I hope you found it both novel and helpful.

But things are about to get harder on the separate self and the illusion spurred by a belief in it—the ego. So if you're ready, consider the merits of this somewhat meandering proposition:

Any "constructive" activity (working hard, serving others, taking personal responsibility, communicating clearly, building a family or team culture) strategically engaged in for the purpose of another activity (making money, feeling good, attracting followers, coming together, winning a championship) is a step away from who you are. A step away from Source. And this step away prompts another step away, and another and another.

Don't get me wrong. My message here is not that certain activities are good or bad. It's the perspective from which these activities are taken. Ego-based "outward" or "quest-like" activities perpetuate a wild-goose chase of seeking. One after the other, they try (and fail) to cure the tension cultivated by the misunderstanding that the ego is an actual entity that can, in truth, be relieved of tension or find peace.

To end this exhausting cycle of seeking (assuming, as I said, you're ready to end it), you must deprive the ego of its fuel. Not through more outward activity, which further enables the ego while veiling who you are. To end the activity cycle, you must go right to the heart of who you are. You must turn your attention inward.

Said another way, since there's no actual step toward the true Self—toward Consciousness, or Source—an inward exploration forces the ego out of activity and into quiet, into stillness. The ego then fades. Now you're home. Answers abound. Actions are instinctive. Energy is conserved. You are free.

You've tried and tried the exhaustive search outward. Isn't it time to hold still and call the ego's bluff? To fold inward? To be the most passionate, productive, and loving you? To be who you truly are?

The unburdened answer: Yes.

INDUCING INDEPENDENCE

Once while taking a walk, I noticed something that I'd describe as heartbreaking. A woman was attempting to teach her young son independence. The little boy was crying, and his mother, in an apparent attempt to impart resilience, mental toughness, or tough love, was slowly backing away.

She said, "Now don't you cry." And the boy was trying, but the tears kept coming. It brought me back to my first summer at overnight camp when, as a first grader, I cried myself to sleep each night for two months while faking a stiff upper lip during the day.

But why? Why would this well-intentioned mother, as do many parents, put her son through a forced separation?

The answer is that our culture conditions us to believe that inducing independence, at any age and in all walks of life, is necessary when it simply is not. Attempting to teach children (or anyone) that they're an independent entity is, quite frankly, among the most perilous of mistakes because there's no such thing as independence (separation).

That's the reason this youngster was crying. Children don't yet know themselves as separate. They know we share a Being, a singular Being. That nothing exists apart from the whole. That as the whole, they are whole. That there are no "me" and "not me." So, when programmed to believe themselves to be what they can never be (independent or separate), children and then teenagers spend much of their time trying to cope. They do this, and we've all been there, by turning to objects, or vices, in a debilitating quest to overcome their confusion, fear, and subsequent tension.

It turns out, as I'll continue to reveal, that not inducing or focusing on independence is what fosters happiness. It's what inspires secure and resilient children to grow up to be secure and resilient adults. It's what allows the true Self to rest peacefully and purposefully as itself.

I'd also be remiss if I didn't add that love is never, ever tough.

HOOKED ON A FEELING

In self-help circles, the advice to "look for and find a good feeling" is common. And for obvious reasons. Who doesn't covet a "good" feeling? Relief, comfort, security. In fact, that's all the little boy's mother was trying to find as she schooled him on independence.

And yet, when exploring who you truly are (investigating the nature of experience, breaking down belief, coming to know eternal peace), please consider that a good feeling is not the place to look. A feeling is not the thing to get hooked on.

The reason:

A feeling is not who you are.

Feelings are objects. Like all objects, they are transient, impermanent. They come, they go, they provide no lasting guidance. Not to mention that seeking a good feeling, absent of an experiential understanding of your true nature, is at the heart of addiction—where respite is found, lost, and then the cycle repeats.

Our intention is different. On this journey, we eliminate the mix-up that aids and abets seeking a feeling. We see through the illusion or primary belief that "I am a limited and lacking separate self." As you know, the belief in a separate self is rampant, as are the intention and activity of trying to feel good, which are propagated by this belief.

The guidance here is basic:

Rather than seek or get hooked on a feeling, and irrespective of any discomfort that arises within, keep exploring who you are.

Find what does not come and go.
What does not share the limits and destiny of the body.
What cannot leave you.
What is not an object.
Get hooked on that.

YOU'VE FOUND YOUR CAPTAINS

Early in my career, I was asked to talk to a college football team one afternoon during training camp. Prior to my talk, a motivational expert addressed the team. I arrived just in time to hear the expert's intense speech about self-belief, connection, communication, body language, mental toughness, and the many personal hardships that he had "tenaciously" overcome.

Then I watched as almost the whole team yelled, screamed, and acted a bit crazy as they ran onto the field. All but two senior players.

I turned to the head coach, grinned, and said, "You've found your captains."

IN OR OUT?

We're well into section 1, so a status check:

Where would you now say that the world appears? Within you or separate from you?

I ask once again because, well, I understand. At times, the state of the world has you troubled. You hunger to help both the world and yourself. But let's be certain you can. Let's be certain your starting point is true, your foundation solid.

After all, if the world appears separate from or outside of you, and duality and the cause-and-effect it espouses are *true*, then fixing the world in order to fix your troubles would make sense.

But . . .

If the world appears within you, and duality and cause-and-effect are *not true*, then fixing the world in order to fix your troubles would not make sense.

Which is it?

Indisputably, our culture was founded on the premise that the world does appear and exist outside of us. And so, we keep trying to fix, control, stockpile, or modify the content of experience in order to find comfort.

But—and I'll keep asking—how are we doing?

Are we living in compassion? Are we living in peace?

Not exactly.

Could it be that our culture's founding premise is backward?

Could it be that rather than continuing to search for and find comfort in objects (substances, activities, accolades, relationships, and states of mind) we should merely ask ourselves if we've ever even experienced a world, or anything, outside of ourselves?

No one can truthfully answer yes to that question.

And if nothing has ever been found outside of ourselves, doesn't this mean that everything—the entire world of objects, others, and events—appears within and is made of ourselves?

Could this be the simple reason why we keep spinning our wheels? Why we keep trying to fix the circumstances of the world but keep moving further away from compassion and peace? In the history of humankind, we've tried everything except considering that the world just might be made of the whole (or Consciousness).

Why not consider it?

Let's put the seeking of solutions on the back burner and explore and understand the essence of Being. Our shared Being. The non-dual nature of all apparent things. Let's consider the possibility that we're trying to fix "things" that don't exist as we know them, and then consider the implications of this possibility.

For starters, here's an interesting implication:

If we are made of the whole, which is infinite (has no edge) and eternal (has no expiration), then we don't need to be fixed.

Are you in or out?

TAKING A STAND

Here's hoping that you're in. That you're becoming more interested in the exploration of Self and the essence of reality.

Not for the purpose of saving the reality within—the Self doesn't control what arises and dissolves—but simply out of curiosity, out of interest, out of wonder.

What, then, are you overlooking about reality? You experience the widespread tension, and disharmony, that appear so real. And while this tension might be occasionally interrupted as you try a new "fix" or advance a new cause, you can't deny that no solution has endured.

Ask yourself:

"Why do I keep seeking to relieve myself of tension, or to

change my reality, when doing so has a 0 percent record of success?" You, like almost everyone, seek relief in objects. Heck, you even follow other objects, or embodiments of tension (insecure gurus), believing they have the answers. You teach your children to seek relief outside of themselves too.

But what if, rather than looking at a world outside of yourself, you truly are looking at a world—a reality—within?

What I'm highlighting is that "look within" isn't some sweet-sounding metaphor. Right now, you *are* experiencing people, places, and events that indiscriminately arise and dissolve within yourself and are made of yourself. Just as the contents of a dreamer's mind are made of that mind, you are looking at your very own insides. You are experiencing the inner workings of yourself.

What I'm asserting, too, is that this alone is what we're overlooking.

Give this a try:

Even if you're still questioning, even if tension is lingering, take a stand here and now as the Being in which all experience occurs and out of which all experience is made. No running from or fixing yourself, or your reality, allowed.

Then, as you continue through these pages, gauge whether this perspective (you are the whole looking within itself, not a person looking outside of himself or herself) is *just* a metaphor. Gauge whether this perspective takes effort, or whether it takes effort to be, or try to be, a separate person.

My suggestion, once more, is that we have the foundation of reality in reverse.

THE TRUE SELF AND THE PERSONAL CAN NEVER MEET

Since who you are is the reverse of who you've been trained to think you are, a few quick rules of the road:

- An exploration of the true Self will not help you find a good feeling.
- An exploration of the true Self will not help you overcome an addiction, improve performance, save a marriage, or make more money.
- An exploration of the true Self will not help you for any personal reason.

Yes, you can uncover who you are, see through the lens of who you are—Consciousness, or love itself—and be in the world from this perspective.

But love is not personal. Feelings are not personal. Achievements are not personal. No experience occurs on behalf of or through a person.

You are and always will be the reverse of what's personal.

NOT EVEN THESE WORDS

I cannot say it enough. Never believe what someone says or writes. Not me. Not anyone. Not the words in this book.

Check in with experience. Your own experience.

For instance, just because Viktor Frankl* claimed that we control our attitude no matter the circumstance, in your experience, is this 100 percent accurate? Just because the Dalai Lama alleges that the practice of compassion leads to happiness, in your experience, is this correct? Just because many self-help experts insist that positive thoughts bring positive feelings, in your experience, is this even possible?

To be fair, what these references are missing, what we overlook when we adhere to these words or types of teachings, is the context in which they were said. Perhaps Frankl was pointing to the illusory nature of circumstances or other objects, and "control" was an added allowance or concession based on the current understanding or perspective of his audience.

We'll never know. Here again, though, is why we mustn't blindly adopt or believe what anyone says.

Is the credo you live by, share, or teach built on belief? Or is experience the bedrock?

It's worth a look.

STAY TRUE

Think back a few notes to "The Difference" (p. 39), where I presented the stark contrast between my approach—self-exploration, self-discovery, etc.—and the prevailing self-help model. I now present a somewhat whimsical example of how this difference tends to play out:

I was once interviewed by the agent of a pro golfer who was

*Frankl (1905–1997) was an Austrian Holocaust survivor, neurologist, psychiatrist, philosopher, author, and a person I greatly respect.

interested in working with me. Right off, I gave him my standard terms that my work had nothing to do with results or helping his client achieve personal success.

"I heard about your terms," the agent interjected. "What's the reason for them?"

I replied, "The no-BS reason?"

"Please."

"This probably won't all be clear to you, but once I realized that players don't actually exist as we believe they do, and that mindsets, golf tournaments, trophies, money, and prestige are not what we believe them to be either, it became nonsensical and essentially fraudulent to treat players and other objects as I had done before. It was now obvious to me that all things are just images or transient vibrations within the whole."

I paused for a response that didn't come, then continued:

"For it to be logical to pursue personal achievement, including the clarity of mind that some players want my assistance with, a player or person would have to be capable of achieving what he or she seeks. But since all things are made of the whole, and the whole is all there is, this 'capability' is an illusion. My role, because of this, is to help curb aimless seeking. To reveal that there are no separate objects *to* seek. This revelation, the revelation of no separation, is the essence of peace, love, and happiness. The essence of self-discovery."

Finally, he responded, with perhaps a bit of a test:

"Will this revelation help him be more charitable, nicer with the fans, even be more considerate to his wife?"

"I refer you back to my terms."

"When can we start?"

NOW MORE THAN EVER

When you get right down to it, there are but two motivations for your, or for anyone's, actions:

- You act in order to seek who you are (peace, love, happiness).
- You act in order to express who you are (peace, love, happiness).

Regarding the first motivation—which applies to nearly all of your actions—here's a suggestion:

Turn this seeking inward. It's always more helpful to not seek peace, love, and happiness in objects. (As a reminder of what I briefly explained in the Introduction, I define an *object* as anything that is known—a possession, achievement, relationship, career, thought, feeling, or mood.)

You cannot find who you *are* in who you *are not*. You cannot improve or upgrade who you *are not*, an object, in order to find who you *are*. Trying to locate the true Self by turning away from the true Self is impossible. And, as we're witnessing with the desperate seeking of objects in our world today, it can also be perilous. The world is in conflict.

Intention matters.

Is your intention to find yourself in objects or to lose that need? Only the latter allows you to express yourself, and be true to yourself, fully.

Now more than ever, it's vital to inquire, "Who am I?"

THE OLDEST TRICK IN THE BOOK

You know the trick. It's born from intention gone awry. As I did in the distant past, you've likely employed it a time or two as well.

It's the duplicitous (though innocent) psychological trick used by salespeople, ad agencies, motivational speakers, self-help professionals, medical professionals, way too many preachers and politicians, and anyone seeking to gain control.

What is the oldest trick in the book?

> *Fortify separation and the fear inherent in this belief, formulate a problem or enemy to overcome, and then provide and take credit for the cure.*

To demonstrate, courtesy of an email that I received promoting a self-help seminar, here's a common way that one's services are sold:

> For each of us in our own personal way, life today presents all sorts of challenges. These challenges bring insecurity, stress, and worry. But, thankfully, my simple approach to insecurity, stress, and worry has proved life-changing for me and for others. Now you, too, can finally find the sustained peace of mind you've been after. In fact, people return to my seminars year after year to reignite their sense of connection and purpose. Book your place today!

In other words:

Step 1. Ingrain the belief that we're separate beings viewing life from a perspective of separation.

Step 2. Rightly confirm that this belief and perspective bring insecurity, stress, and worry (fear).

Step 3. Provide the "cure"—an approach, distraction, affirmation, or connection strategy—for the separation and fear (the enemy) just ingrained.

Step 4. Generate a high of hope, a temporarily improved feeling.

Step 5. State that for the high to continue you must come back for more.

Here's a different idea: Let's say we altogether abandon this oldest trick.

How's that accomplished?

Step 1. Explore inward. Discover that we're not separate beings.

Step 2. Recognize that feeling fear is an attribute of separate beings, not of who we truly are.

Step 3. Understand that because we're not separate beings, we don't need to cure fear. Improved feelings or highs are not essential to who we truly are.

Step 4. Appreciate that because we're not separate beings, a separate being (a self-help professional) can't change or improve us.

Step 5. Come back for more? We're OK, but thanks.

One more thing: If you, in your life or work, are fortifying the fear inherent in the belief that "I am a limited and lacking separate self" and offering illusory cures for the fear that *you* just fortified, and this note is rubbing you the wrong way, then good. It should. Maybe it's time to reevaluate your intentions and get to know yourself.

As I said, you may be innocently employing the oldest trick in the book when it comes to your career, relationships, and other life situations. But the true Self? It wouldn't dare.

THE CRUDE PRAYER OF MATERIALISM

While we're on the subject of reevaluating intentions, I define the crude prayer of materialism like this:

> *A prayer from a separate or personal self, to a separate or distant God, for the intention of obtaining a separate or distinct object.*

This prayer can never be answered.

There is no separate self, God, or object.

Prayers can only come true when the one praying, the one prayed to, and the intention of prayer are all the same.

Only then will we know ourselves.

WHY SHARE?

About ten times a week, I receive an email comment like this:

> Garret, your point that there's no such entity as a separate self or body is delusional and obviously incorrect. If your extremist positions are true, then why do you (a body) share emails with us every week? Why help anyone? Why share anything?

Here's why:

Because the obliteration of the belief that "I am a separate self or body" does not negate the appearance or illusion of separation. Knowing that separation isn't real does not bring an end to the appearance of separate selves and objects or to the appearance of living in a world of separate selves and objects.

By way of analogy, recognizing that the pools of water that appear in a desert are mirages does not stop them from appearing. The pools still appear, but their reality is now known.

To reiterate, when you no longer believe yourself to be a separate object, you will still experience the illusion of a world of separation.

But you are no longer *of* that world.

And further:

Because you now understand that you don't possess the limits and destiny of an object (a separate self or body), defenses crumble; the need to protect fades away. You're now in the world as the true Self, as love, as that which has no limits or destiny. You point away from all that is personal. Away from a reliance on or need for fame, fortune, proper states of mind, security, or the existence of separate others. You surrender. You're open. You share without caution or effort. Come what may.

TRAINED TO SEEK

Way back when my friends and I were in school, here's what was shared with us—or, I should say, drilled into us:

Confidence is key.

So we searched and searched for confidence, failed to find it, and turned to any method under the sun to acquire this elusive trait. More training for sports, more fights, more girls. For some, drugs or booze. A few of my friends were even suspended from school for behavior that stemmed from seeking the confidence that our school's teachers and coaches had strongly urged us to seek.

And today?

While teachers and coaches appear to have refined the message, while they appear to have tamped down the need to seek outward for traits like confidence, they're still encouraging the same, only it's now disguised as something different.

Many, for example, tell our youth that it's an "inside job." That everyone is born confident and happy. That well-being is the natural state of a person. That wisdom, resilience, and security exist inside each of them—"in their bodies," that is.

But here's the thing:

As it was with the claims of my teachers and coaches, there's no evidence whatsoever that any of today's claims are true. What's the plan when those told that they own well-being, wisdom, resilience, and the rest can't find these traits within a personal self? Should they just keep seeking? The very suggestion that we own something within ourselves is what initiates the seeking for that particular something. And alongside seeking, suffering will always arise. As will damaging behavior. Absent of seeking what can't be found, the true Self is revealed.

Perhaps, then, my teachers and coaches were the ones seeking.

Perhaps, advice-givers today are the ones seeking.

Perhaps, in an innocent quest to continually fix our own suffering, we're training a future generation of seekers.

Has seeking well-being, wisdom, resilience, or security brought us well-being, wisdom, resilience, or security?

Perhaps instead of perpetuating this maddening cycle, it's up to us to break it.

OUR KIDS

We teach our kids, right out of the cradle, that they're each a separate self. That they're personal specks, isolated and individual, within a universe of a trillion other specks.

On top of that, as you've just read, we teach our kids the importance of self-confidence. That while isolated and individual, they're also meant to be secure.

The contradiction is glaring. How the heck can an isolated and individual speck be secure?

No wonder our kids grow up dazed, confused, and dependent on seeking relief.

We can do better.

And we will.

A TRUE PARENT

The day I stopped indoctrinating my own children with the cultural beliefs that I was indoctrinated with, the beliefs that kept me in limitation and lack, the beliefs that shrouded the true Self, was the day that I'd say I became a true parent. This was the day I became a mentor, role model, and welcomed resource for my three children.

Ask yourself:

"Am I passing down the same generational conditioning that has me suffering, seeking relief, experiencing relief, suffering again, and on and on?"

It's never too late to turn yourself around. To pivot toward Source. To dismantle your conditioned beliefs. To be the true you. Then, and only then, can you help your children (or anyone) be themselves, so they may shine as who they truly are too.

COURAGE

The dismantling of beliefs, I won't deny, takes a whole lot of courage. It's not easy to challenge and then change your parenting, your teachings, the examples you set.

Do you have the courage to challenge the things you believe in, the lies that govern your life? The standard belief catalog includes:

- "I am a lacking human being who needs *x*, *y*, and *z* to make up for my lack."
- "I am a limited human being who needs *x*, *y*, and *z* to make up for my limits."

- "Thoughts, feelings, and sensations occur within my very own body, so I need them to be *just* right."

It's OK if you haven't yet mustered the courage. We've got much more ground to cover.

But just so you know, what remains upon the dismantling of beliefs will essentially be what you were attempting to find by adhering to them.

What remains will be peace.

What remains will be harmony.

What remains will be true.

START TODAY

Like you, everyone has sensed, at one time or another, that there's something more to themselves and to life than meets the eye.

Like you, everyone would also admit, if they're upfront about it, that seeking to unravel or quell this intuitive sense in a world of objects (where we've been trained to seek) has perpetuated confusion and more seeking—which has everyone caught in a seemingly endless cycle of pleasure and pain.

But if delving further into the object-based world (the material world) is not the overall answer, where else should you look? What else should you do?

Here's a gentle suggestion:

Rather than move toward objects, hold still.

And here's a not-so-gentle suggestion:

Right where you are, start here. Start now. Whatever you have planned for the rest of today—a job to complete, people to meet, a leisure activity—avoid connecting your identity to it. Avoid seeking comfort in it.

In fact, avoid seeking in the object-based world entirely.

How will you know if you're seeking?

Simple. Insecurity. Seeking and insecurity go hand in hand. Insecurity is an intuitive warning that you've taken yourself to be limited and lacking. You've taken yourself to be an object seeking other objects. You've ignored your true essence.

Oh, I get that it won't be easy to refrain from seeking in the object-based world. Conditioning is formidable. Yet that's where an ace in the hole that you might not know about comes in: a community of fellow explorers who no longer succumb to the belief in separation, in duality.* When one gets lost in a world of objects, these fellow explorers step up, providing love, support, and an unwavering guidance back within.

There's no step from you to you. What you're looking for—what we're all looking for—won't be found until seeking for yourself in a world of objects has ceased.

CHARACTERS

Do you want to achieve "great things"?

That's cool.

But before you try, here's a different take on achievement derived from the perspective that separation is illusory, that all things are made of the same essence, of Consciousness. I refer to this perspective as the "Consciousness-only" model.

*If you're interested, reach out through my website, garretkramer.com, and I'll make the intros.

As I've detailed, you've been taught to believe yourself to be a person. A separate character with a date of birth, name, and place of origin. Of course you weren't born thinking that "I am this person or character." You've simply been conditioned to experience life from this standpoint.

What's more, this rather abstract character is fulfilling a role. Among fellow characters, it's living a life that, like a dream, is unfolding as it will. But due to your conditioning, you've likely forgotten that it's a dream. You think this character is controlling itself and can alter this unfolding. So you're trying, you're pushing. Life seems serious and short. You sense burden and pressure. You want to achieve, but this effort is not bearing fruit. And you worry that you're destined to get nowhere.

Truth be told, that was my worry too—until many years ago, when I encountered my friend and mentor, a character named Richard Carlson (author of the *Don't Sweat the Small Stuff* series and other books). While supporting my desire to achieve, Richard reminded me of who I was, of my lack of control, and of what was actually going on.

I'm now reminding you of the same:

From the illusory or conditioned perspective of a character, the dream appears real. Life appears real. Control appears real. From the actual perspective of the dreamer (the true Self), however, it's all a dream. It's all Consciousness. The notion of control, or that there's a separate controller, is utterly foreign. Not even the dreamer controls the dream.

Back to the question at the start of this note. Does your character still want to achieve great things?

If yes, again, that's cool.

But is your character at peace and in harmony? Is your character unburdened? Is your character capable of giving all it's got? Is your character ready and able to achieve?

Those questions require a more thorough examination. Because to answer yes to those questions, your character's role must be to live life to the fullest while simultaneously understanding that it's all a dream and that there's no such thing as control or personal achievement.

Is that you?

Are you poised to overcome your conditioning? To boldly live and love with all your heart as if nothing is on the line? Are you free to "achieve" those things?

No need to reply. Keep reading. The dream is unfolding right now.

NO SEEKING, KNOW PEACE

Are you seeking to fix . . .

- A feeling?
- A weakness?
- Negativity?
- Self-centeredness?
- A lack of confidence?
- An addiction?
- Prejudice?

- Loneliness?
- A disease?
- Global warming?
- Hate?

What you seek to fix, you perpetuate.

Desire arises not as a call to seek fixes, but as a call to hold still. A call away from the world of objects. A call inward. A call to intuition and effortless resolution.

No seeking fixes. Know well-being. Know peace.

THE EGO IS CUNNING

In regard to seeking, there's no more cunning ploy of the ego (recall that the "ego" results from the belief that "I am a separate self, a limited and lacking object") than this: seeking clarity, serenity, or any state of mind.

Seeking in feeling-states will appear to be more constructive or even more spiritual than seeking such objects as fame, fortune, or success. But a state of mind, too, is an object. And, as described in the last note, seeking in a world of objects is the surefire path to the perpetuation of trouble.

THE UNFEASIBLE AND INEFFECTIVE MODERN TECHNIQUE OF "DOING NOTHING"

Are you acquainted with the suddenly in-vogue and zen-like technique of telling a person mired in trouble or difficulty, a sufferer, to "do nothing" and let the system self-correct in order to overcome suffering?

I've come across nothing less effective. Honestly, it's madness. Doing nothing is not to be mistaken for holding still and folding inward. In fact, offering do-nothing advice to someone just might bring you a good smack to the head. (Maybe from yourself if you try to follow it!)

Here's why:

A sufferer is incapable of doing nothing. Much like insisting that someone in an agitated state relax or calm down, if a sufferer were capable of doing nothing and simply letting suffering pass, or allowing a feeling-state to heal itself, then that sufferer wouldn't be suffering in the first place.

In addition, "do nothing" is still doing *something*. Similar to taking a pill or thinking positive thoughts, it's a coping technique designed to resist suffering.

Do you really want to help a sufferer?

Why not do this? Investigate who it is that's suffering. Check out where suffering takes place. Get curious about what suffering is made of. No distractions ("doing nothing" is one of those). No substances, gurus, books, videos, or other forays into the object-based world. No running away from yourself. No trying to rid yourself of suffering.

Hold still and explore. Allow the mind to fold inward.

For example, answer these questions (and go slow with them):

Can suffering be found independent of a body? Without the belief that "I am a separate self residing in a body," does suffering even exist?

And, speaking of the self . . .

Has a separate self ever been experienced? Has a self ever been found independent of other selves or objects, or outside of the room, environment, space, or universe in which all selves and objects appear?

You know the drill. Of course not.

So if there is no independent self or individual, no tangible ego, could there possibly be a suffering independent self or individual? Is "doing nothing" in order to rid a nonexistent separate entity of suffering even a relevant consideration?

Why, then, try an unfeasible and ego-based technique that (as is the case with all coping techniques) holds misunderstanding and suffering in place when *doing something*, namely a little bit of self-inquiry, a turn toward Source, is all that's necessary?

A SIX-MONTH STUDY

From the audience at one of my talks, a counselor once presented me with this proposition:

A six-month study of two groups of twenty people. One group would receive counseling, therapy, or life coaching—in other words, coping techniques. The other would explore non-duality, self-realization, the Consciousness-only model. He assured me that after six months the data would show the first group to be "by far" more at ease.

I replied to the counselor, "You might be right. But people becoming more at ease or comfortable is precisely the reason I'm not interested in your proposition."

Why this reply?

Because what gives rise to the craving for comfort and the

seeking of it through modalities rife with techniques, and then to interminable cycles of pleasure and pain, is the belief that "I am a person or separate self."

Self-exploration, unbeknownst to this counselor, is not undertaken for the purpose of acquiring comfort. It's to eliminate the belief in separation and, with it, the need to seek comfort.

IF YOU DIDN'T KNOW, YOU WOULDN'T SEEK

As we home in on the basis of seeking, mull over this:

In the recesses of your mind, you know who you are. Among the words used to describe who you are: *Consciousness*, *Source*, *God*, *Awareness*, *I am*.

There's but one reason you seek these descriptions: a longing for true nature, a calling home, the knowing that "I cannot be a separate self."

You seek who you are because you know who you are.

MENTAL HEALTH DAY

The topic of mental health, sorry to say, is a distraction from who you are—the true Self—if there ever was one.

And while World Mental Health Day is now marked on the calendar each year, my question to any expert on mental health or anyone promoting this day is:

Where would one's mental health be found?

It's the most serious of questions. There's a lot of suffering, sickness, and conflict around. Those promoting this day are certainly trying to help.

But are they?

Perhaps mental health can't be found.

I mean, where in the body would it be found?

Perhaps (as I'll address next) this is what's known deep down and why so many prefer to avoid discussions around mental health.

And not only that. Perhaps seeking mental health—good feelings, some vision of innate well-being, security, or resilience—is the very root of suffering, sickness, and conflict.

After all, no human being is actually secure or resilient. Human beings are transient images that appear within the whole and then dissolve back from where they came.

Perhaps it's understanding who we are, and not mental health, that we yearn for.

Perhaps the promotion of World Mental Health Day, or a discussion and examination of mental health in general, precipitates the so-called "mental health problems" that we're trying to solve.

Again, where would one's mental health be found? If human beings could find it, wouldn't that have happened by now?

Have you found mental health?

Perhaps it's time to call off the search.

THE STIGMA

Let's dig further into this illusive attribute known as mental health. Mainly, the stigma (and shame) referred to in statements like this:

> *Mental health is a subject that most people feel embarrassed to speak up about.*

That statement is then frequently supported and amplified with another like this:

> *We all face challenges in this regard. Low moods and insecurity aren't things to hide. Let's encourage each other to be brave and seek help when we need it.*

But let me just say right here that this stigma is nothing more than a conditioned belief. A belief that, like all beliefs, you need not subscribe to. Experience tells me that we're no more embarrassed to speak up about this issue than about any other issue.

Rather, staying with experience, what really keeps us from seeking the guidance of mental health professionals is the general methodology of their profession. It's centered on treating, fixing, coping, controlling, or managing the psyche or separate self. Deep down, we know that something about this methodology doesn't add up. We know that a separate self, by nature, is a transient or insecure image. We know that attempts to fix insecurity are made in vain. We know that from the limited perspective of a separate self (or according to the misunderstanding that we are separate selves who are limited to bodies and minds), insecurity is fundamental.

So I'd say we should be commended—not stigmatized—for our refusal to seek help in a methodology built on misunderstanding. I'd say we're right to avoid any methodology that attempts to make a body-mind secure. We're right to not try to treat temporary sensations of fear and lack. We're right to turn away from experts who proclaim that something is wrong if we don't feel resilient, stable, or mentally tough.

You know as much as anyone. Don't let others convince you that you need to be fixed or that you lack mental health. You cannot lack what doesn't exist. You cannot escape insecurity. But you can explore and come to recognize the body-mind for what it actually is—a transient image that comes and goes within the whole we call Consciousness.

Our spiritual journey through *True Self,* the folding inward toward the true Self, reveals an entirely different perspective on the body-mind, insecurity, the illusion of mental health, and more.

DESIRE AND GRACE

It's now worth mentioning yet another remnant of the belief that we are separate entities who lack:

We attempt to use a spiritual teaching or understanding for personal gain, as an explanation for why things happen, or as a mechanism for good feelings or comfort.

This, my friend, is not spiritual. It's materialistic.

Spiritual materialism—employing God, or Consciousness, as a means to a personal end—is common. But it's born from desire (seeking), not grace (being yourself).

Be with failure. Be with uncertainty. Be with struggle.

With grace, spirit takes hold.

IN THE HANDS OF CONSCIOUSNESS

While having dinner one night with my friend Grayson Hart, a pro athlete in the UK, our conversation turned to the topic of sleep.

This topic comes up often. Athletes can't escape today's glut of information on the importance of getting sufficient sleep. Regrettably, this information isn't helping them fall asleep (it's the opposite). So they sometimes look to me for guidance.

Grayson claimed, "The more I get myself to drop the thoughts in my head, the faster I fall asleep."

I replied, "Since when are you personally responsible for dropping thought, for falling asleep, or for anything? If the experience of dropping thought and falling asleep arises, it arises. If it doesn't arise, it doesn't arise. Everything that occurs is in the hands of Consciousness."

Grayson then wondered, "You're suggesting that we don't have the power to voluntarily clear our heads or fall asleep. I get that. But, back to sleep, what about steps to improve it? Are you saying that I shouldn't take them at all?"

"No. Carry on as you see fit. But if you take steps to improve sleep, this experience is arising within Consciousness. If you don't take those steps, same deal. Whatever you do, again, is in the hands of Consciousness. Frankly, all aspects of experience—including actions and outcomes—are fleeting images or configurations that Consciousness has effortlessly assumed at those particular moments."

"Hmm, I've just seen something," Grayson whispered. "And as I do, I sense a wave of peace."

"Me too, buddy. But let's not fall asleep in our soup!"

ASK YOURSELF THIS

What do you know for certain?

I don't mean something you've learned like 2 + 2 = 4, that you belong to a nationality or religion, that positive feelings beat negative feelings, that government laws or mandates must be adhered to, that both circumstances and your thoughts can make you upset, that money is valuable, that personal prosperity trumps the welfare of those less fortunate, that the separation you see is real, or that you were born and will die. I mean, what do you know beyond a shadow of a doubt, *for certain*?

As section 1 of this book has demonstrated (fingers crossed), there's no question more important. It's but another form of "Who are you?" And I ask this question to every person I work with, speak to, and love.

While at first glance it might seem benign, this question will essentially rock you and your world to the core. It will disintegrate your conception of self. It will blow apart the presumptions and opinions of others—the beliefs—that you've unknowingly accepted as true and live by. It will render your conditioning, the programming or indoctrination of our culture, powerless.

In fact, if during your read through the rest of this book (and beyond) you hold your attention on this question and the pathless path toward truth it evokes—if you avoid the lure of personal comfort, aggrandizement, or trying to rid yourself of insecurity and fear—you will no longer know yourself as a limited, lacking individual. If you keep asking yourself this question until each and every belief or ingrained falsehood is gone, it will become clear that you are and always will be complete. It will become obvious that life is viewed from the opposite of a personal or separate perspective. There will be no doubt that the entirety of experience is on behalf of, one with, and made of the infinite and eternal whole we call the true Self, Consciousness, or God.

You've been called to discover that which cannot vanish. To discover who you are not, and who you truly are.

Regardless of what arises and falls within you—peace, love, and happiness will, now and forever, endure.

THE SEAMLESS NATURE OF EXPERIENCE

My intention, as we move to section 2, is to keep challenging your belief system, or what you think is true. To encourage you to face your long-held beliefs and see them for the falsehoods they are. To ask you to ask yourself if the basis from which you're living your life has been taught to you rather than arrived at through your own direct experience.

Consider this note, then, a recap of what we've spoken about so far. With an added twist.

From a young age, we're all taught that reality is defined by separation, by the lines of distinction we perceive. That the universe consists of separate selves and separate objects. That human beings exist separate from each other. That trees exist separate from the rest of nature. That clouds exist separate from the sky. That all things exist separate from all other things.

But, again, what if the opposite were true?

What if the foundation of perception is a unified and infinite canvas with no distinctions? (Imagine a photo of a landscape becoming blurry to the point of nothingness.) What if reality is fundamentally indivisible, complete, and inexhaustibly abundant? What if separation, or duality, is no more than a culturally conditioned belief? What if everyone and everything were modulations or vibrations of the whole?

What a different world it would be.

I know it's still nearly impossible to grasp. Our conditioning fully overwhelms us. But let's keep exploring, let's keep inquiring. There's so much more to upend.

What if, since the conditioned mind or intellect can't grasp the seamlessness of experience, Consciousness (or God) spontaneously brings objects into apparent form? What if Consciousness generates lines of distinction by vibrating, contracting, and localizing within its own infinite canvas? What if, along with appearing to conceal Consciousness, "separate objects" are actually revealing Consciousness?

That explains why perception seems to be something it's not. Without this contraction of Consciousness, how would manifestation be perceived at all? And while manifestation can be glorious and its distinctions—people, trees, clouds, and the rest—splendid, manifestation has also brought consequences. It's come at a cost. We've taken these lines of distinction, these objects, as genuine. Instead of mere images made of Consciousness, we've presumed objects to be significant and valuable separate entities made of matter. We've succumbed to the illusion of duality. Materialism and greed are ruling the day.

This will only be the case, however, until the day it is not.

If the very premise of *True Self* is accurate, indeed what a different world it would be. Separation, division, and inequality would be flagged as the irrational beliefs they've always been. Nature would remain unscathed. Money, food, and water would be amply and equitably distributed.

Just as vital, knowing that lines of distinction are illusory and merely brought into temporary focus for the benefit of manifestation would become the priority, the sole source of and impetus for our behavior. Knowing that we share a Being, harmony would bloom.

Finally, if you're so inclined, before we move on to section 2, try this exercise that I often use with teams, audiences, and performers:

From where you sit or stand right now, focus super hard on the various objects that come into view. Find lines of distinction. Divide, separate, judge. Establish duality, materialistic preference, or hierarchy.

And then, don't.

Simply see. Sense. Have an experience. Allow the indivisible and seamless nature of the whole to take you where it will. Allow the transparency, the sameness, the intimacy of all things to completely consume you. Envision that you're looking inside yourself, at a world made entirely of yourself.

So which perspective is real? Which perspective is true?

Not sure? You'll know it via your direct experience. The heart prevailing over the head. Innocence beaming through indoctrination. When an unlimited, cohesive, and borderless canvas is experienced, only the true Self remains. We cease searching for our identity in objects, in others, or in anything from the material world. The material world then ceases to be an actual world.

Now we are free. Now we are true. Consciousness pervades.

What do you say at this point?

Still game?

Rather than the current object-based, or materialistic, model, perhaps a Consciousness-only model is worth serious consideration. Rather than finding your purpose in the activities, titles, careers, or relationships of the material world, perhaps your sole purpose—the knowing of your own Being, the knowing that "I am Consciousness"—is to be expressed *through* the activities, careers, and relationships of that world.

Thank you for being open to it. Thank you for staying with it. Thank you for reading this book.

Further inward we go.

INQUIRIES AND ANSWERS

How is it that I'm not a separate self?

All objects—including people—appear within the whole. There can't be an outside of the whole, and there can't be an object separate from the whole. So you can't be a separate self. Separation is an appearance or illusion.

Who or what, then, is experiencing this conversation? This is what we continue to explore.

Why does everything you write seem so contrary?

Our culture has presumed that experience takes place from inside a body, that a person is the one who experiences. From the perspective of this misunderstanding, everything experienced will be backward.

I've heard you say that behavior occurs indiscriminately, or out of our control. But you also say that it depends on our conditioning. How can both be true?

Do we control our conditioning? As with all experiences, conditioning, as well as its impact on behavior, occurs indiscriminately.

What's an example of pregame or preshow advice that you might offer?

I've sent this simple text message more times than I can count: "If you knew for certain that failure was just a conditioned belief, what one word would best describe your approach to today's game or performance? Don't tell me. Take your answer and be that! Express that!"

You discourage seeking. If I'm not seeking to improve, learn, get fit, or help others, then what am I supposed to do in life?

You touch on an important topic. Without a doubt, the nature of one who believes himself or herself to be a separate person is to seek. That's why the implication here, so to speak, is to "seek" who or what you truly are.

In other words, we could provisionally describe self-exploration as inward seeking, as surrender, as holding still and exploring inward. It's your purest and only true calling because when you stop seeking "outward," the belief in separation vanishes. From a perspective of wholeness (the perspective of the true Self, of Consciousness), you're then in a selfless position to dive into the world and, rather than seek, express love and serve.

My boyfriend left me. I'm so miserable. Can you help?

I'm sorry. I'll do my best.

Misery, or suffering, stems from these three descriptions of the same habit: resistance to current experience, seeking a better experience, or connecting one's identity to the content of experience. This habit is programmed into us. Into you. It's not who you are, however. Quite the contrary.

Experience actually reveals that what arises, even a breakup, cannot harm who you are. I'm not saying it will be easy, but as you explore the essence of who you are—as programming diminishes—your eternal (resilient) nature will become clear. And while you might not yet appreciate what arises within you, these modulations of you will soon be seen in a whole new light.

What's the best way for performers to deal with nervous feelings and find peace?

This is a common question that reaches beyond the performance arena. Over the years, there have been so many techniques designed to distract us from feelings that it's easy to lose track. And while these techniques may seem to have an immediate effect, they have no staying power.

The answer to your question is to simply face and welcome the feelings that arise while performing. Do not run from or try to cure them. We'll then find the eternal peace we were innocently and mistakenly seeking.

As I've said many times, we can't find peace, or the true Self, by distracting our attention away from it.

If there's no such thing as separation, why do you bring up resisting and seeking as the causes of suffering? How can one thing cause another thing if they are not really separate?

For ease of understanding, especially at an early stage of the teaching, I speak of resisting current experience and seeking a different experience as the causes of suffering. We've been conditioned to take separation at face value, so I'm making a concession, an allowance, for this conditioning.

But suffering will soon be seen not as a separate, and awful, thing as we've been taught. It will be seen for what it truly is:

a modulation that arises within the whole, made of the whole (Consciousness).

Why is it unproductive to try to change thoughts and feelings?

All objects, thoughts and feelings included, arise and dissolve within you. You've never experienced a thought or feeling arising and dissolving anywhere else. That being the case, thoughts and feelings aren't separate from you. They're not foreign invaders. They're one with you. The substance of thoughts and feelings is you.

Trying to change or exchange thoughts and feelings is an exercise in futility. Positive, negative, whatever—all thoughts and feelings are already the same.

Is your work meant to fly in the face of the self-help industry and even psychology?

Not intentionally. But any industry that seeks to help or comfort the separate self, or to legitimize the belief that "I am a separate or personal self," is advancing the misunderstanding that underlies all misfortune. By contrast, an exploration of true nature—my work—is about challenging the belief that we're a culture of separate human beings. It's about going directly to experience.

Have you experienced a separate human being (or any object separate from or outside of the whole)? Do you experience from the perspective of a separate human being? Our culture, including the self-help industry, keeps seeking new frontiers and methods. Trouble is, our culture is oblivious to who we are. Does it not follow that from a defective foundation, we'll just compound confusion and suffering?

Do human beings own a psychological immune system? Do our minds self-correct, as you said in your last book?

No. I was wrong about that. While it's sometimes claimed that human beings have this inbuilt power, what you're referencing, and what I was referencing in that book without knowing it, is the sensation of relief—which results exclusively from the cessation of searching for happiness in the material world.

What does "shared Being" mean? Who or what shares a Being? You and I?

Kind of. More to the point, it means that while things appear to exist separate from or outside of Consciousness, I, Consciousness, share my Being with all things (physical objects, people, animals, nature, circumstances). All things exist within and are made of myself.

In the sports world, is there a constant among athletes or coaches that you've noticed?

There are many. This one may surprise you: In the aftermath of a game or tournament—win or lose—those who've set their sights on success are miserable.

Can we discuss "God's will"? I've come to see that free will is more or less a concept, not a truth. But the idea that things happen at the will of God also seems like a reach to me.

Let's first clear up your "more or less a concept" statement. Free will is 100 percent a concept, or not true. You say "more or less" because free will appears to be at work sometimes but not others. For example, while we seem to not be in control of the thoughts that arise, we seem to be in control of or have free will over what we do with these thoughts. Yet, in actual fact, what we do with our thoughts (our subsequent thoughts and actions) can only arise in a similar fashion as our initial thoughts (out of our control).

Now to God's will. This, as you rightly indicate, is also a concept—one that seems to counter or replace free will. Both of these concepts, however, are branches of the illusion of separation. That is, from the illusory perspective of a separate self, it looks like there's a choice between free will and God's will. But from the perspective of the whole, or of God, all things arise within and are made of the whole. There's only God. So what exactly would God, let alone a person, be choosing or willing?

Again, for either free will or God's will to be *true*, separation would have to be true. And it's not. Separation is an illusion.

How can I most productively help someone who's hurting, someone with an addiction or depression? I assume it's to clear up the sufferer's belief that "I am a body or separate self." Is that right?

I'm afraid not. The shortest route is for *you* to see that "I am not a body or separate self." You cannot truly serve, openly and selflessly, until the belief in separation (duality, materialism) is gone. And your question is a sign that it's not yet gone.

So, from here on, make the knowing of your own Being your sole intention. Helping others, like all actions, will become a natural or fluid response to self-exploration.

The term* non-duality *still perplexes me; I just can't relate. What's a comparable term?

Obvious answer: *not two*. More relatable answer, perhaps: *undivided*.

What does it mean to "look to experience"? You say this quite often, and I want to be clear.

"Look to experience," or "this is what direct experience tells me," means exploring the true nature, essence, or reality of experience.

Initially, though, most will take this suggestion from a personal perspective. And that's appropriate and good; it starts the process of breaking down the accumulation of conditioned beliefs.

By way of illustration, have you experienced being born? You assume or believe so. But in truth, the answer is no. You've never experienced the birth of yourself. Have you experienced a sound, or any object, at a distance or separate from yourself? Again, you believe so. But in truth, the answer is no: All sounds take place within you. Ultimately, if you continue to break down beliefs, you'll arrive at what can't be broken down or disproven: You have never experienced the absence of Consciousness.

Looking to experience—direct experience, or the nature of experience before conditioned beliefs—reveals that you've never appeared or disappeared. You are infinite and eternal Consciousness. As are all the experiences that can only arise and dissolve within yourself.

I really dislike a situation involving our team at the moment. I know I'm not seeing it clearly, but I still can't shake this upset feeling. Thoughts?

It's never the initial resistance or reaction to a situation that causes upset. It's the *resistance* to the *initial resistance* that does this. Whatever arises, arises. If you're upset, be upset. Be you. That's it.

Many teachers claim, "No matter how you feel, you're always OK." This has never rung true to me. Is this what you're claiming too?

I'm claiming something different. I'm claiming, or revealing, that the one who knows feelings doesn't feel feelings. That you, Consciousness, are the ever-present knower of all objects (feelings are objects). That you, Consciousness, are not an object. That regardless of what arises and dissolves within it, Consciousness is resilient, eternal, always OK.

If a teacher is ascribing resilience to a person—a transient and nonresilient object—you're right to question it.

You opened up a recent talk by advising us not to believe anything, including what you say. Do you believe what you say?

I don't. In order to believe, there would have to be a separate believer and a separate something to believe in. Duality would have to be real. As we've explored and reviewed, duality is an appearance or illusion. It's not real.

This is not to infer, however, that we don't drop down off the perch of purity in order to share, communicate, and explore who or what we are. So here goes: If we look to our direct experience, we find that, rather than it being a belief, it's true that an object cannot appear separate from or outside of the whole called Consciousness. It's true that any sense of separation is illusory. It's true that we don't experience on behalf of or through a separate self (a body). And, given that, it's true that all experience is on behalf of who we are—Consciousness.

Is there a tip you favor for getting rid of anxiety?

The next time you're tempted to apply a tip to rid anxiety from yourself, don't. You can't rid anxiety from yourself. Where would it go?

Rather, see if you can pinpoint the precise location of anxiety in the body. If, in fact, the sensation belongs to the body, you'll be able to locate its epicenter. Once you can't locate it, get curious: "I know this sensation is located within me, so then who am I?"

Not the body. All sensations arise within the true Self, within Consciousness. And this realization, not the personalization of anxiety, allows anxiety to melt back to the nothingness from which it came.

Objects appear not outside of me but within me. I get that. At least, I think do. But do objects appear within you too?

Your statement and question shed light on the grip the belief in separation has on you. You're presuming that *you*, a separate self, is addressing *me*, a separate self. And that objects can somehow appear within separate selves. This presumption, however, is contrary to your experience.

If you examine direct experience, you'll find that objects appear and disappear within the whole (or Consciousness). Where else could they appear and disappear? And you are this whole, the knower of objects. All objects appear and disappear within you. This includes the object that is whomever you're speaking to.

All that's truly known is your own direct experience. Stick with that and the grip of belief won't stand a chance.

Earl Nightingale* said, "Success is the progressive realization of a worthwhile goal." How do you define success?

Happiness. The knowing of your own Being. Causeless joy.

As you've written, "Thought does not create one's reality." But if that's the case, what does?

Indeed, thought does not create one's reality (or feelings, or anything for that matter). There's no creator of creation. Creation just is.

You raise an interesting point, though. So let's look at the foundation of this belief: materialism, the theory of a separate subject and object, or what might also be called cause-and-effect. As kids, we're taught to seek a cause for things. We're conditioned to find a creator. That's why, rather than simply accepting our reality as is, we claim that human beings did it, or God did it, or that thought creates one's reality, when our actual experience reveals that the content of reality arises and dissolves for no reason at all.

---

*Earl Nightingale (1921–1989) was a radio personality and author who focused on personal development and motivation.

Cause-and-effect—which requires a "creator" standing separate from its "creation"—is a concept. It's not a truth. For there to be a separate creator and its creation, a creation would have to exist separate from the whole (and be made of something other than the whole). This separation has never occurred.

What would you tell a teacher, coach, or counselor who's starting out?

Explore and set aside your beliefs one by one until you arrive at what can't be set aside, that which is immovable, permanent. You will have then found yourself, you can then be yourself, and you will then be ready to serve.

I'd also add that every mistake I've made in my career, the things I was incorrect about, resulted from me not heeding this advice. I defaulted to my beliefs at times of uncertainty, to what others had told me was true. Always explore for yourself and you'll avoid this pitfall.

You seem to not be an advocate of the self-help industry. How come?

This isn't easy to say, and I'm not blaming anyone, but no industry gaslights more than the self-help industry. This industry suggests that we lack—we should be more positive, determined, grateful, clear-minded, creative, selfless, etc.—and then asks us to spend money to cure a sense of lack that didn't exist until the industry suggested it.

When it comes to helping a so-called "other," the self-help industry overlooks the most important of understandings: "I am not a separate self; I am not a body and mind; I cannot lack."

Beyond the preeminent purpose of knowing who or what I am, do I (and each of us) have a unique and identifiable purpose in life?

No. "Find your why" mantras are ego-fueled distractions. Your true purpose, as you allude, is the knowing of your own Being. Efforts to feel good, succeed, have a family, win games, buy nice things, become famous, or even save the world are all well and good, but they're veiled attempts to discover who or what you truly are.

Because you are not personal, you cannot seek, arrive at, or possess a personal purpose. You, the true Self, are God's infinite Being. You are yearning in life to know yourself.

Does it take time to lose the belief that "I am a separate self"? It seems as if my intellect gets it, but my senses are slow to catch up.

In almost all cases, the belief that "I am a separate self" dissipates gradually. But it's important to note that once this belief is gone, the illusion of separation remains. And this is the "lag" you describe. We forever see or sense separation. We now understand that it's not real.

Why do you downplay the importance of having the proper attitude or state of mind, and the importance of working hard to achieve it?

If you're holding on to the conditioning that the proper attitude or state of mind is important, then it will make sense to work hard to achieve it—hire mind coaches, read books on the subject, attend seminars, and on and on. But if you know that an attitude or state is merely a transient and powerless sensation, you won't feel the need to work on it. You'll simply stick to the project at hand, whatever that project may be.

Rather than trying to feel better, what's proved beneficial to me is understanding how I work psychologically. Or, "As I think, I feel." Do you discount this?

I don't discount anything. But what you're stating is a belief. And beliefs are neither a substitute for nor a confirmation of experience.

First, and candidly, if you weren't trying to feel better, you wouldn't analyze the supposed cause of feelings. Second, if you truly yearn to understand, then instead of understanding how you work psychologically, isn't it reasonable to first understand who you are? Because if you get who you are incorrect, then you'll also get how you work incorrect.

Who am I? Do I experience on behalf of or through a body? What do I know for sure? Whereas these questions are at the heart of curiosity and understanding, "how" and "why" questions (How do I work? How does the mind work? Why do I feel this way?) are at the heart of confusion. In fact, upon ascertaining who you are and what all things are made of, "how" and "why" questions will fade. As will the need to feel better.

What's the aim in teaching us about true nature/non-duality?

There is none. The recognition of non-duality is the aim. All actions are undertaken with the intention of uncovering our true nature. This, or returning to Source, is actually everyone's aim, the basis of all desire, our sole purpose. We overlook this fact because we overlook that we are one Being longing to know, or unveil, our Self.

Do you have thoughts on the tactic of "distancing" yourself from your thoughts, feelings, or even others?

Any suggestion to tactically "distance yourself," while innocent, is ignorant, as the suggestion is ignoring the fact that distancing is impossible.

Have you ever intentionally tried to shun yourself from something or someone? My guess is that it didn't work out so well. Reason being: Objects don't appear separate from, outside of, or at a distance from you. *Here* you are, and the objects of experience (thoughts, feelings, sounds, smells, people, situations) are *here* too. You cannot distance yourself from something or someone that can only appear in the presence of yourself.

I'm so all over the place and anxious right now. How can I find calm amid the storm?

Start here: Are you certain that you are anxious? If you were "so all over the place," how would you know the feelings you so keenly described?

Anxiety comes and goes within you. But you do not come and go. Although you experience anxious feelings, you never change or become these feelings. You yourself are never anxious.

What is truth?

It's what remains after everything you believe in has vanished.

2.

The Knowing of Self

To know yourself truly, you must boldly begin anew. You must be willing to explore for yourself, and then explore some more. You must be willing to not adhere to the opinions of others. You must be willing to consider that the primary presumption or belief, "I am a separate self," is inaccurate. You must be willing to consider that you do not undertake any action or task on behalf of or through a body.

As a matter of fact, you've never even experienced an object—an apparent world, other people, animals, or circumstances—on behalf of or through a body. A personal experience, a human experience, is all made up.

Are you, here at the outset of section 2, still doubting the essence of experience? Do you still think that "I am not a separate self" is just another alluring, trendy, or perhaps outlandish idea?

Not your fault. The belief that "I am a separate self" or "I experience through a body or separate self" is pervasive, so much so that the truth is almost always neglected in favor of some self-improvement or self-aggrandizement method. But be honest.

For as long as you can remember, you've jumped from one of these types of methods to another, yet insecurity and distress still beckon for relief.

In light of that, let's continue our gaze toward truth. Let's explore the essence of experience, the knowing of Self, and then let's explore some more.

- You can, of course, experience a wide array of objects. You can experience events. You can experience thoughts and feelings. You can experience sensations and perceptions.
- You can, of course, experience bodies or separate selves—friends interacting, children playing a game.
- You can, of course, experience a body that supposedly belongs to you partaking in activities such as interacting with friends or playing a game.

But a body that "belongs to you," like all sensations and perceptions, arises within the whole. There's no evidence of any kind that this body is the one who experiences, that this body equals the true Self. (As an aside, the sensation of a hand running up an arm to a shoulder, to a face, to the eyes, is just that, a sensation. The perception of darkness when the eyes are covered is just that, a perception. Both arise within the true Self. Experiment with this if you'd like. Do either sensation or perception irrefutably take place from the standpoint of a body?)

Again, to know who you are, you must summon the nerve to question the very beliefs that obscure who you are. You must question the lies that feed insecurity and distress, the lies that veil the truth. Obliterate the primary presumption—the belief that "I, a separate self, am the knower, the experiencer"—and the entire structure comes crashing down real quick.

Who am I?

Not a body.

I am the one who knows.

The one who experiences.

The one in which all things appear, and out of which all things are made.

To know yourself, to uncover eternal peace for you and the world within, you must get in front of conditioning and learned labels. You must see with fresh eyes. You must boldly begin anew.

That is the plan for this section.

THE ONE THING

With respect to expanded exploration into the knowing of Self and new beginnings, here's a new inquiry:

To be something, wouldn't you have to experience that something always, without interruption?

You cannot, for instance, be that which appears and disappears, arises and dissolves, or comes and goes. You cannot be that which is not eternally with you, there for you, or present.

What's the one "thing" that satisfies all of these prerequisites? The one thing you always experience? The one thing that's never been absent? The one thing that cannot disappear or disappoint?

That one thing is not an object. It's not a belief, thought, mood, substance, activity, or relationship. It's not the body or mind.

That one thing is Consciousness.

Know yourself as Consciousness. You will have then found your Self.

THERE COMES A TIME

There comes a time when the knowing of your own Being, Consciousness, becomes the priority.

There comes a time when peace, love, and happiness matter more than fame, fortune, and comfort.

There comes a time when freedom displaces fear.

There comes a time when truth is spoken at the risk of ridicule.

There comes a time when you stay with experience and don't try to fix it.

If that time hasn't come yet—no worries, it will.

THE PRODIGAL SON

One day, the prodigal was "unhappy." Trying to improve his feeling-state, he ventured "away" from his father, away from home.

He sought and gathered up as many objects of the material world as he could.

Then, one day, buoyed by the absence of interference from his father, the prodigal son realized that what he longed for couldn't be found in the material world.

He did an abrupt about-face. He turned around and journeyed inward. He journeyed home.

He soon found what he longed for back home.

TO COPE IS TO MISUNDERSTAND

Your efforts to cope (resist or seek) are made in the absence of understanding.

If you're deliberately resisting an experience or seeking to find a better one—attempting to change a thought, attempting to manage a feeling, attempting to alter the dynamics of a relationship, attempting to acquire more stuff—you're failing to understand the nature of experience.

Why?

Because, by definition, to try to fix an experience, to cope, is to misunderstand that all experiences happen within you and are made of you. With this understanding intact, what would there be to fix?

To demonstrate, perhaps there was a time when you thought, like the prodigal son did at first, that the experience of unhappiness could be swept away with the help of an object (perhaps you still think this to a certain extent).

But once you understand that unhappiness is itself an object, once you understand that the objects of experience are transient illusions made of the whole, once you understand the nature of experience, trying to fix unhappiness becomes ridiculous. I mean, you'd obviously have a hard time trying to fix an illusion, much less replacing an illusion with another illusion.

Hold still. Like the prodigal son did in the end, fold inward. Familiarize yourself with yourself.

Who are you?

All that you've been resisting and seeking is precisely who you are, where you are, right now.

WITHIN ME

While it's now likely obvious that objects can only appear within the whole—within the universe, within Consciousness—here's what might not be obvious:

Thoughts ("I am unhappy") and feelings (unhappiness) are also objects.

Like all objects, thoughts and feelings are known.

This is not inconsequential. Because of the confusion over the nature of thoughts and feelings, we first assume or believe that thoughts and feelings appear somewhere separate from where other objects appear. Then, because thoughts and feelings obviously "appear within me," we believe that thoughts and feelings appear "in here," while all other objects appear "out there." We believe that "*here* is me, my body, and *there* are all other objects, including other bodies, that are not me." We believe that "I am not the universe, not Consciousness; I am a separate self or body."

Bogged down in this belief system or misunderstanding, confusion and suffering then reign. Relief is sought and provided. But because this relief (in the form of therapies, strategies, etc.) is based on the same misunderstanding of being separate, it's temporary at best. Ultimately, under this misunderstanding, survival of the "fittest" separate self, discrimination, and conflict become the rule.

On the other hand, what if this belief system, this misunderstanding, were erased altogether? What if we were to truly "begin anew" as I offered? What if we understood that "I am the universe, infinite and eternal Consciousness, and all objects appear within me, are one with me, and are known by me"?

Well, here we are.

WHERE THOUGHTS APPEAR

As revealed throughout section 1, our conditioning is strong. So, rephrasing the questions and conclusions of the previous note, let's stay on the topic of our conditioning a bit longer.

Where do thoughts appear?

If you still say within your head, fair enough. But how do you know this to be true? Have you ever found a thought in your head? (Or, for good measure, a feeling in your finger, a sensation in your gut, a perception in your eye?)

No. To have or be a body is itself a thought, and a thought cannot appear within another thought.

Again, where do thoughts appear?

Still difficult? It's OK. Where thoughts appear is not itself an object. The mind can't pinpoint it.

But consider this:

Just as the blue of the sky is untarnished by clouds, birds, planes, lightning, storms, or any object, where thoughts appear remains untarnished by any and all thoughts.

Less difficult, yes? Let's follow this further with another question:

Why is it important to understand that where thoughts appear cannot be harmed by thoughts?

Simple. All of us have spent a good part of our lives resisting or seeking to change what's meant to come and go in the first place, to such a degree that we've never considered that where thoughts appear is not within a body or mind. And, along with that, where thoughts appear does not share the limits and destiny of a body or mind.

In other words, in our focus on cognitive fixes, we've completely overlooked that thoughts (feelings, sensations, perceptions, and all objects) are transient, while where they appear (and disappear) is resilient, permanent, eternal.

Once more, where do thoughts appear?

We've discussed it. Thoughts appear within you.

And who are you? You can't be a separate person. Separation is not real.

You are the universe. Consciousness itself. Or, if you prefer, Awareness, or God's infinite Being.

Whatever name you choose, or if you choose no name at all, it's just essential to know that the space where thoughts, even stormy ones, appear remains unaffected by whatever comes and goes within it.

You are the deep blue sky. You are that space. Whole, pure, untarnished, come what may—forever.

A VARIETY THAT DOESN'T EXIST

There's further conditioning to rectify on the way to the knowing of Self.

Are you ready?

A variety of feelings—highs, lows, and the like—doesn't exist. A variety of feelings is a belief.

Not as far as you're concerned?

That's why I asked if you were ready. Again, based on the conditioning of our culture, it makes sense that you wouldn't relate to my claim.

Yet what if the primary cultural belief in separation, the belief that you are a separate self, were completely eradicated? What if, as this book proposes, infinite and eternal Consciousness *is* who you are? And since objects—including feelings—can only appear within you, they're made of you too? Wouldn't that mean that the essence of all feelings is the same?

Based on that premise, let's commit to this:

In spite of a culture, or civilization, that's intensely focused on feelings, a culture that encourages the analysis of their meaning, a culture that's got us seeking the good and running from the bad, a culture that's trying so hard to feel better—let's leave feelings for another day.

And in its place, consider again (and again) the question:

Who are you?

For if you get that question incorrect, as I've mentioned, everything downstream, such as your understanding of feelings and what to do or not do with them, will also be incorrect.

Sure, like all distinctions, a variety of feelings (as well as a hierarchy of feelings) will seem real.

But *knowing* eclipses *feeling*.

And the fact that feelings are nothing other than Consciousness in disguise is all that you—Consciousness—need to know.

RATHER THAN FIX THYSELF, KNOW THYSELF

Nevertheless, if you believe yourself to be a person, a body and mind, then it will remain a given that you'll attempt to rid yourself of certain feelings. Pain or discomfort, in particular. People, modulations within Consciousness, are fixers by nature. They cannot allow, surrender, or leave things alone.

But a guarantee:

Once it becomes clear that you are Consciousness itself, rather than a modulation within Consciousness, allowance and ease of response will become a given. Consciousness is simultaneously one with and free from whatever moves within. It does not discriminate. It does not detect enemies. The totality of experience is welcomed. No object is dodged or denied—not pain, not discomfort, not anything.

Know thyself. Make that your aim.

You will then intuitively, not personally and fearfully, respond to any and all experiences.

"ONE WITH"—THE MEANING

For years, I struggled with the meaning of these spiritual assertions:

- All things are made of the same substance or essence.
- Look within for the answers you seek.
- You are what you seek.
- Separation is an illusion.
- Who you truly are does not share the limits and destiny of the body.
- I am one with all things.
- I and my Father are one.

If you, too, have struggled, then let's now explore their meaning together.

And to begin, I'm going to ask you once again to imagine the vast space in which all things appear . . .

That's right, the universe.

As you know (or as far as you know), no object has ever been found outside of this space. No object has entered the universe from somewhere else or exited to somewhere else. There is no "outside" of the universe.

As you know, no one has found an edge to the universe. It is infinite.

As you know, while within the universe objects seem to change, grow, wither, appear, disappear, live, and die, the universe does none of that. It is eternal.

So far so good?

Cool.

But let's slow down a bit. Because even though we've covered this already, our exploration and the following questions are about to get more direct as we put this issue to bed.

If all objects are contained within this infinite and eternal space we're calling the universe—and, again, there's no outside of the universe—wouldn't this mean that all objects are made of the universe?

Still tricky, yes? That's because you've been deeply conditioned to see all things, including this exploration, from the perspective of an object, a body, within the universe. So, instead of that perspective, let's finally take a stab at viewing this exploration from the perspective of a universe that can only look within itself.

As I said not too far back, you, my friend, are the universe. And because those objects (thoughts, feelings, people, circumstances) you see or sense have never appeared anywhere but right where you're looking, wouldn't this verify that the entirety of objects is appearing within one universe, one Consciousness, or you? That all objects are simply modulations of the universe within the universe? That all objects are made of the universe? That all objects are the universe?

Let's circle back. What do you make of these assertions now?

- All things are made of the same substance or essence.
- Look within (Consciousness, not the body) for the answers you seek.
- You are what you seek.
- Separation is an illusion.
- Who you truly are does not share the limits and destiny of the body.
- I am one with all things.
- I and my Father are one.

And to complete the list . . .

- I am the universe.

Conditioning be damned.

TRY THIS FIRST

Before spending one more second trying to clear the mind as you've been conditioned to do—which, as experience (the antithesis of conditioning) reveals, is an endless pursuit—pause and ask yourself about the mind's true essence. Explore the nature of this mystery called "mind."

Then, once you realize that a mind, a tangible mind, can't be found, that a mind doesn't exist as anything other than an idea or concept, allow the culturally conditioned belief in "mind" to dissolve. And with it, the conditioned belief that the proper mindset (clarity, peace of mind) is essential.

What remains will be what you were attempting to acquire with and through the mind. Not the proper mindset. What remains will be infinite and eternal Consciousness. What remains will be peace.

THE ONE WHO KNOWS

While I obviously don't recommend that you try to clear the mind, I do recommend that you now take a genuine look—a look not jaded by belief—at the one who *knows* a mind, as well as all objects.

What I seem to know at the moment, for example, is the computer on which I write as well as the rest of the apparent objects of my office.

These objects are known. In other words, these objects are not me. I am the knower of these objects.

And what else is known?

I know the sensation of fingertips on keys, of ankles crossed, of a left instep pressing the floor. I sense, imagine, and experience an entire body or object named Garret that sits in a chair.

And I also know thoughts—of confusion.

Why confusion?

Because I had believed Garret to be the knower of objects. And now Garret is an object among other objects that's known. How can this be?

Indeed, years back, this very confusion was the first apparent bump in the road in my exploration into the nature of experience. Into the essence of the knower. Into the revelation of who I am.

Now this road bump, this intriguing confusion, is here for you.

You've lived all this time under the primary presumption that the body, a mere object with a name, is the knower.

But, again, is this presumption true?

"I am the body." This thought, idea, or concept, like all objects, is transient. It appears, and then—while reading, while playing a sport or a musical instrument, in deep sleep, or in moments of extraordinary passion and beauty—it can't be found. In the wake of these moments, "I wasn't the doer" and "I lost myself" are familiar refrains.

So these questions:

Who is the one who knows that the body wasn't the doer? Who is the one who knows that the body was lost or can't be found?

Not the body. The body can't know its own absence.

Which leads to these questions:

Who does not come and go?

Who's not an object?

Who is the knower of all objects—computers, thoughts, minds, bodies, and even the absence of these things?

You've *known* the answer unquestionably, without interruption, forever and ever: "I am the one. I am the knower."

You were taught to believe that "I am" implies the body. But experience says no.

The knower is not the body. You are not the body. You are not transient.

Who you are is ever-present, permanent.

Who you are, the true Self, can only be Consciousness.

ARE YOU CONSCIOUS?

How about supersmart people, say, neuroscientists? Do they grapple with questions such as "Is the body the knower?" "Are human beings conscious or aware?"

Not really.

Neuroscientists, like most people, tend to believe, as an absolute, that human beings are conscious. Or that Consciousness is a property of the body. What neuroscientists do grapple with, and have for decades, is trying to find the neural connections that give the body and brain the power to think, know, experience, decide, and control.

In short, neuroscientists yearn to know where personal consciousness (note the lowercase *c* denoting the personal) is found.

Not surprisingly, they've had no luck. Neuroscientists can't pinpoint these neural connections, let alone the localization of personal consciousness. And so they're confronted with what's been classified as "the hard problem of consciousness"—the hard problem being that they can't figure out how a body made of matter produces consciousness. What they don't understand is that it doesn't. A body is no more conscious, or aware, than a rock, thought, or any object. Only Consciousness is conscious. Only Awareness is aware. The true Self (Consciousness, Awareness) is itself the knower.

That is, because neuroscientists think that a human being is the one who knows or experiences, think that the body and the true Self are one and the same, they're searching for a personal consciousness that doesn't exist. They're looking within the body for answers that can't be found there.

Most neuroscientists, then, have the entire formula in reverse. Consciousness has become quite the mystery. And while a scant few are catching on (check out the work of Bernardo Kastrup), this book, with a bit of luck, will help right the ship.

After all, experience shows that we're not splintered-off fragments or separate conscious beings. Experience shows that there's no such thing as an actual separate being, no such thing as an actual transient object, let alone a conscious one. Experience shows, over and over, that the true Self equals Consciousness. That all "beings" are images, modulations, or vibrations within and made of that which is permanent and secure.

BREAK FREE FROM THE PACK

Here's a brief refresh of something that, in one way or another, I won't stop dwelling on:

Insecurity doesn't arise as a result of failure. It arises when we link our well-being and identity to success.

Life is to be played, not won. We play music. We play sports. We play games. We play characters.

Insecurity, when it arises, is simply asking you to break free from the conditioning of our culture. This is the conditioning that has you seeking yourself—your OK-ness, your purpose—in acquisitions, admiration, and predominately through "success." This is the conditioning that also has you believing that you're a conscious separate being, a person with a limited existence, that needs other objects in order to become whole.

You haven't fully listened to your insecurity.

It's still there.

But not for long.

THE WRONG TURN

What happens when we're valiantly trying to cure insecurity or any apparent disorder—addiction, anger, famine, bullying, discrimination, mass shootings in the United States, pollution, a global health crisis, war—and don't realize that we've taken a wrong turn?

We keep going and going, traveling further away from both the spot where the disorder materialized and the solution.

This, alas, is where our culture is at today. It explains why the same disorders that plagued the world two hundred years ago plague the world right now. We keep applying fixes, keep acquiring information, keep fighting for what each seemingly separate person experiences and thinks is right, and we haven't caught on to the fact that a separate person has never *had* an experience. Not one single time.

The primary wrong turn was believing that experience is viewed on behalf of a person, body-mind, or human being. And this continues to be the road we're traveling. Although this belief is not valid.

What do you say we backtrack? In this note, let's go way back to that initial point of reckoning.

There we stood at this metaphoric cultural intersection.

To the right: "I am" . . . a person, body-mind, human being.

To the left: "I am" . . . the true Self, Consciousness, God's infinite Being.

We went right. We should have gone left. We presumed "I am" to be a separate self. The belief took hold. We've been living the lie of isolation—and painstakingly seeking comfort, wholeness, and connection—ever since.

Can you experience (perceive or observe) a separate self who is experiencing these words?

Is the one experiencing these words a person or object in a world of objects?

No and no.

"I am" the true Self. Not a person or object. And these words, like all persons and objects, are happening within me. They are made of me. They are experienced by me.

Not fully there yet?

That's fine.

We'll keep backtracking as we go.

PASSION AND GRIND

Passion and *grind* are believed to be synonyms. But not so fast. As I've done with many performers, let's backtrack on this subtle but destructive belief.

Passion conserves energy. Grind spends it.

Passion is effortless. Grind is strenuous.

Passion is free. Grind is burdensome.

Passion is an effortless expression. Grind is an in-built warning.

In other words, grind—toil, hard work, and exertion too—is a sign to ease up, a sign that you've overlooked who you are. Which then allows passion to come shining through.

THE TRUTH AND THE WAY

In the arenas of self-help, coaching, and counseling, the word *truth*, like the word *passion*, is also commonly muddled and then depreciated:

- "It's true that I'm a hard worker."
- "Live your truth."
- "I'm truly heartbroken."
- "The truth is that in sports, the home team has an advantage."

And then, as none of these types of claims are accurate (true), the use of the word *truth* is sometimes snubbed:

- "No one really knows what's true."

- "Truth is a mystery."
- "Who are you to say what's true?"
- "Words can never accurately describe truth."
- "Your little mind can't know truth, so don't bother trying to find it."

Sound familiar?

But the thing is, while beliefs (both lists) are personal, truth is not. Everyone knows what's true. The truth is so basic, so unpretentious, so ordinary, that it's hiding in plain sight.

What's true?

Don't take my word for it. I've written this note and this book to help you initiate your own exploration. But here you go, once more, in slightly different words:

- Nothing has been experienced outside of Consciousness.
- Nothing has been experienced other than Consciousness.
- Nothing has been experienced by something other than Consciousness.

Consciousness is the essence of all objects. We've never known its absence. Consciousness has never turned off. Consciousness has never run out. Consciousness has never left our side. The truth, on that account, is that we are Consciousness. One Being. All images, all objects, appear within us.

And, frankly, it seems a shame that the truth is so plainly hidden. A shame that exploration in the direction of truth is avoided and sometimes discouraged or even disparaged.

Why a shame?

Because the essence of Being—knowing that all objects within our shared Being, or within Consciousness, are made of the same "substance," knowing that this substance makes up an indivisible whole, knowing that hard lines of separation cannot be found, knowing that we are infinite and eternal—is the true starting point of honesty, compassion, and all moral behaviors. It's the only means through which we can do unto "others" as we'd have them do unto us. It's the only way the world will find peace.

The knowing of our own Being is likewise the only path for harmony and trust in our marriages, families, friendships, teams, companies, and communities. It must be the foundation. A life built on the shaky ground of materialistic beliefs and pursuits—such as connection (why would what is not separate need to connect?), communication (to whom would what is not separate communicate?), managing feelings or moods (what are feelings and moods made of?), survival of the fittest (what are *we* made of?), or even the worshipping of a separate God—is essentially doomed to collapse. Beliefs and pursuits are personal. They're not based on the foundation, the truth, that we share a Being. One Being.

And further, without recognizing this foundation and abandoning these types of materialistic or personal beliefs and pursuits, not only will a marriage or team collapse under its own weight, but eventually, everything will. Materialism is a paradigm of disunion, of conflict. It's a paradigm of taking from people, animals, and nature in order to benefit a separate "me" that doesn't exist.

As I've said, don't take my word for anything I just claimed or for any claim in *True Self*.

Keep contemplating for yourself. Discover the nature of reality, the veracity of experience. Keep reading, keep exploring until you strip bare all of your beliefs and arrive at the only thing left standing.

Then explore some more.

The implications of truth are infinite.

PROOF

Proof, or evidence that something is "true," is an essential ingredient in virtually all aspects of our culture. It's required in science, in criminal investigations, at border crossings, to diagnose illnesses, to obtain certifications, and in pro sports since the advent of instant replay.

But think back to the very beginning of section 2. As detailed, we have no proof that the presumption or belief that underpins our culture is true. No proof that a human being is the one who knows, thinks, or experiences. No proof that separate human beings exist as anything other than modulations, or you might even say personifications, within and of the whole. And if we've gotten wrong who we are, if we sit back and accept the primary belief in separation, everything that follows will be inauthentic, illegitimate, all messed up.

This is the reason I wrote this book. And while throughout my career I've been labeled "completely nuts" more times than I can remember for not sitting back, for questioning the primary belief, for not following the crowd, what seems really nuts is an entire culture or civilization built on belief rather than on proof or authenticated experience.

Let's reexamine this inquiry:

"Can a separate self who's experiencing these words be experienced or found?"

Proof of this would be direct evidence that there exists a human being who is reading these words right now. Proof of this would be direct evidence that *you* are a separate self. As I've asked before, can you find evidence of that? Can you observe a separate self with your given name reading this book? I don't mean the hands holding this book. Can you witness the actual circumstance of yourself reading it?

Of course you can't.

So where's your proof?

You've just been conditioned to believe that who you are—the reader of these words, the experiencer of the world—is a person with your name. Yet proof that you are this person doesn't exist. In fact, this very belief that our culture insists we have proof of is the only thing for which we have no proof. We've got the true Self totally mixed up.

To reiterate, you are indeed experiencing these words. You are indeed experiencing a world.

You, the true Self. You, Consciousness.

Now look up from the book. The one object that can't be found is the object or person you've been trained to think you are. You're looking within yourself, at the inside of yourself. You're experiencing the appearance, or illusion, of separate objects made of yourself.

There is no true separation, there are no true separate objects, there is no true separate you.

Prove me wrong.

ON RESEARCH

Bear in mind that proof—or direct experience—is not the same as research.

Research (a diligent investigation and collection of data especially aimed at the revision of accepted theories and laws) merely tells us how the apparent thing being researched *apparently* works. It does not tell us how the thing truly works or what it is made of.

Take, for example, the theory of positive thinking. Research declaring that the act of replacing a negative thought with a positive thought leads to a positive state 85 percent of the time does not prove the efficiency of this act. It proves the inefficiency of it. Why? Well, if the act caused the state, it would happen 100 percent of the time. So while on the surface research seems to support the theory of positive thinking, it actually shows that positive thoughts have never been the cause of a positive state.

More important, anytime you try to prove cause-and-effect—the aim of research—what you're essentially doing is corroborating the greatest of cultural myths: separation, duality, materialism, the presumption that we're not a singular Being. This is because for one thing to cause another, there must be two separate things. And there are not. So while many are trying to use research (trying to prove cause-and-effect) to cure the afflictions of humanity (end environmental degradation, prevent illness, eliminate conflict), they're effectively doing the opposite. They're fortifying the illusion of and belief in separation, the very foundation of the afflictions they're attempting to cure.

Research, I will acknowledge, does have proper applications—in sports, certain aspects of medicine, and elsewhere. But research cannot prove what's real or what's true. Our culture has been research-driven for as long as anyone can remember. We're even taught that unless they're backed by research, the most mind-blowing inklings and revelations must be rejected. But are we at peace? More benevolent? Healthier? Why keep relying on a faulty direction?

Research requires a look "outside." The word is derived from the Middle French *recherche*, which means "to go about seeking." It's a venture into the mirage of a separate material world.

That's not what we're up to on this inward venture. Our exploration is one of direct experience. Let's, then, be crystal clear about where, according to experience, all things arise: within. Let's keep our attention, and intention, on the nature of

Consciousness, the true Self, the essence of who or what we and all things truly are.

Answers are found nowhere but there. And we don't need research for that.

THE FOUNDATION

Is it becoming clearer that the fragile foundation of your existence, of our collective existence, is belief?

Some beliefs are obvious: "I stink at this or at that." Some not so obvious: "I belong to a nationality, religion, or race." And some almost completely shrouded: "I share the limits and destiny of a body, because I was born and will die."

No doubt, most people are simply going about their business believing what our culture has told them. Without realizing it, they're living lives built upon labels whose "truth" is unsupported by actual experience. They have no idea that the primary belief, "I am a separate self with a limited shelf life," is what gives rise to all other beliefs. To all seeking. To trying so hard to become safe and whole—what they already are. And to all suffering.

On this exploration (as I just indicated regarding research), we take a stand as the opposite of belief. We go to the heart of experience. In this book, "I am infinite and eternal Consciousness" is the foundation.

You've never experienced the absence of Consciousness. It is ever-present, effortless, and knows no bounds. So, with Consciousness as your foundation, dive right into life. Play the game. Serve. Be the best version of yourself. With Consciousness as the foundation, you're on solid ground.

With Consciousness as the foundation, you'll live a life in but not of the material world.

A life of peace. A life of happiness. A genuine life of love.

IT'S NEVER THE THING

- It's never the lover.
- It's never the work of art.
- It's never the activity.
- It's never the setting.
- It's never the job.
- It's never the money.
- It's never the book.
- It's never the teacher.
- It's never the thing.

We cherish the moments. We fall in love. We sense beauty, passion, and purpose. We may eagerly support and serve others.

And yet, these experiences never result from a relationship between subject (a person) and object (see list).

They result from the dissolution of objects—the dissolution of the conditioned beliefs, opinions, and assumptions that have us attributing our experiences (our feelings, our emotions) to objects. From the absence of the relationship between subject and object. From the absence of a separate subject and object altogether. They result from a return to Source.

Surely when our conditioning does creep back in, when we overlook the essence of our own Being, when separation seems plausible, we'll again try to connect a feeling or sensation to an object. But as separation only exists in appearance, a connection cannot take hold. Sadly, the prolongation of suffering (habits, addictions, compulsions, and obsessions) comes solely from accepting as real the illusion of connection.

It's never the thing. You don't need the thing. Who you are, who we are—one infinite and eternal Being that is perpetually experiencing all things made of itself—is always enough.

CAT AND MOUSE

Still, it's normal to feel happy upon finding the "thing." Upon reaching a goal, acquiring an object, learning a new activity, or starting a relationship.

Why is it normal?

Because everyone finds happiness when, for a brief moment, they stop seeking.

But the misunderstanding that the goal, acquisition, activity, or relationship caused the happiness sets up a cat-and-mouse game that perpetuates suffering.

In fact, most of us are addicted to this cat-and-mouse game.

In fact, this misunderstanding is the basis of all addiction.

In fact, the only thing we truly seek, what brings us back to happiness, is to stop seeking.

In fact, we'll remain addicted until we understand that happiness will never be found in the goals, acquisitions, activities, or relationships of the material world.

THE BODY AND RESILIENCE

"Everybody possesses resilience or well-being."

Before you broadcast or share this common self-help theory, as with anything you're tempted to share, make sure your own experience definitely lines up.

Have you ever lost a sense of the body? We discussed it before: While absorbed in a daydream, a book, a movie, while walking in nature, while being intimate, while playing a sport or a musical instrument—has the idea that "I am a separate self" ever faded? Have you ever experienced the absence of objects or selves, the absence of the personal?

Something you lose, something that disappears, if only for a flicker in time, cannot be said to possess resilience, well-being, or any permanent quality.

What *is* resilient, eternally well, and present?

Discover that. Share that. Express that.

I AM

I am that. I am resilient. I am eternally well. I am whole. I am love.

I am the one in which all acts of forgiveness, acceptance, and gratitude take place.

The one in which thoughts, feelings, sights, and sounds arise.

The one who's aware.

But when I try to find the part of me, the part of a body, that has the power to be resilient, to forgive, to think, or to be aware—I can't.

Nobody can or ever has.

That's because I am not a body. A body doesn't know. A body is known. And *I am* that knower. The one who experiences a body and all other things. The one in which all situations appear and disappear. The one out of which all things are made.

Who am I?

I am = God's infinite Being.

I am = Awareness, Consciousness.

I am = the shortest full sentence in the English language.

I am = me, you, us.

THE SOLE REQUIREMENT

Which brings us to the sole requirement. Just like "I am," there's only one. In order to serve, help, or support, in order to teach, coach, or lead—there's but one thing you're required to understand.

It's not complicated. It doesn't take practice or years of study. Right now, the requirement is closer to you than close can be. Deep down, you already understand it fully.

The requirement, no surprise, is this:

> *You must have a sense, an inkling, a clue. You must know who you are.*

Not your name, ancestry, thoughts, feelings, moods, body, or mind. Not your beliefs, values, or ethics. Not your failures, achievements, possessions, professions, marital status, or wealth. Not your personal purpose, race, gender, sexual orientation, nationality, or religion. Who you *truly* are. Because if you don't have a grasp of that, you cannot guide a lost world of seekers back to who they truly are.

Who you are is infinite, eternal, impersonal, complete.

Who you are has the capacity to assume the form of more than 7.5 billion separate selves, plus all objects and animals, and yet always remain whole.

Who you are has the breadth to allow all of life, all of space, all of time to play out within it, on it, as it. And yet, it remains pristine, pure, unscathed, free, and here and now.

Who you are is found between thoughts, in the deepest of sleep, and right at the moment of intimacy.

Who you are has several names, many described in this book, but none of them perfect since who you are predates labels and descriptions.

Who you are is the essence of all experience, that which has never appeared or disappeared, that which remains when everything insecure or temporary has gone.

Who you are seems unreal yet is real.

Who you are is not made of anything, yet all things are made of it.

Indeed, all apparent interactions (whether with friend or foe, whether romantic, platonic, or anywhere in between) are simply who you are, interacting with who you are, in an attempt to travel home to who you are.

Who are you?

You are the Being that you and all seemingly separate objects share.

That's who you are.

You've known it all along.

And that's all you are required to know.

SUFFERING AND NOT, SIMPLIFIED

a. Who you are contains and remains unaffected by objects, others, circumstances, thoughts, feelings, sensations, perceptions, or any experience.

b. When you overlook *a* (the knowing of your own Being, the "sole requirement"), and then resist an experience or seek a better one, you suffer.

c. When you wake up to *a*, and then don't resist an experience or seek a better one, you don't suffer.

Suffering (and I can't overstate this) originates from the ego, which originates from the belief that "I am a separate self." With this belief intact—while oddly also sensing that this belief is not true—you try to control what arises within yourself, all the while knowing in the back of your mind that you can't.

This alone explains confusion. And suffering.

In an attempt to control what arises, you resist and you seek. Even though it's obvious that your attempts to control have never brought happiness.

IF ONLY WE KNEW

As you may recall, I asked a similar question in the very first note of this book:

If you knew that no object existed separate from or outside of yourself, what would the implications be for you and the world in which you live?

I'll now clarify this question.

First, while our culture is built on the belief that objects exist as separate or independent entities, how do we know this to be true? Has an object that exists on its own—exists apart from the one who experiences objects—ever been found? The answer, as evidenced so far, is no.

Second, while I'm not claiming for certain that independently existing objects can't be found, what I'm suggesting is that since this has not yet happened (and I'm not quite sure how it would be possible to find an object without a finder), perhaps it's time we accept that it's never going to happen and explore the ensuing implications.

OK, then. What would be different if we knew that no thought, feeling, person, animal, possession, situation, or environment existed separate from the true Self, separate from Consciousness? *Everything.*

- Politicians would see and be seen with compassion.
- Borders would evaporate.
- Hunger would peter out.
- Abuse of one another and of the planet would cease.

- Greed would not be a thing.
- Enemies would be unheard of.
- People would stop seeking healthier thoughts and higher feeling-states.
- Altruism would flourish. As would peace, love, and happiness.
- Separation would be recognized for the illusion it is. There'd be nothing or no one to hurt.

All that said, do you remain uncertain about the illusion of separation?

Not a problem—that's what our exploration is about.

Would the objects you see, hear, or smell right now be there without you?

Not as far as you know.

They're appearing not separate from but within Consciousness, made of Consciousness, from the perspective of you—Consciousness.

Everything appears within you. And is made of you.

All one and the same.

If only we knew.

Truth be told, we do.

THE MUCH-MALIGNED OPTION

Do you still want the fix? Have you found that you feel better or more secure after implementing a strategy, tool, technique, practice, ritual, or one of the many self-help activities at your disposal?

Many say yes. And while I'd never begrudge your right to reach for a so-called "fix," that won't stop me from repeating the reason why you think you feel better:

Through activities, you're temporarily distracting yourself from the feeling-state called insecurity. This is why specific activities have become staples. Why you keep reading self-help books or watching motivational videos. Why you keep attending seminars, trainings, and retreats.

There is, however, another option. An untaught option. An option much maligned by the self-help world. The option that underscores our journey home:

Know yourself.

Who you are is complete, cannot lack, and doesn't need fixing. Who you are is secure, no matter what arises within.

I'll ask again: Do you still want the fix?

Will you sustain dependence and suffering by seeking it?

DON'T CHASE

Ever notice that the so-called "good things"—peace, love, and happiness—tend to come to you, or fall into your lap, while seeking them tends to leave you frustrated and weary?

There's good reason for this.

In fact, many years ago, when I was an ice hockey forward (whose role was to score), my father used to send me messages demonstrating this interesting phenomenon. He'd say, "Now don't go crashing into the pile around the net. Go soft to the pile and allow the puck to pop out to you."

Today, I often send my daughter, Chelsea (a field hockey scorer), the same type of reminder. Sometimes with a twist like this:

"Who you *are not* is the activity of seeking or chasing objects. Who you are is tranquil, whole, and still. Objects—which are not tranquil, whole, and still—will dissolve into you. Just be you, kid. The game will come to you."

So why do "good things" fall into our laps? Why can we not go to them?

Because the true Self doesn't lack. Because the true Self will not and cannot chase. Because the true Self has no need to chase.

On the contrary, only the ego (the result of the belief in separation) acts from lack, insecurity, or desperation. The ego is drawn toward objects because it requires them to validate its apparent existence. But as the ego's existence is a meager belief, this quest for validation is foolhardy.

Don't chase. Or, as my father would say, "Don't go crashing into the pile." Do the opposite of what the urge is telling you to do. Go soft. Be you. Good things will end up in your lap, or on your stick, in no time.

FATHER, SON, AND EVERYONE

My father, like all people, had his apparent strengths (his timely on-the-mark messages, being the best ice hockey coach I ever saw) as well as his blind spots (he didn't grasp that all criticism is basically self-criticism). Throughout the seemingly thousands of times he found fault with me, for example, he always seemed to be talking about himself. I marveled at this and also wondered why. Now I know: The world we experience is a reflection of our own limitations, of our own ignorance, of the veiling of Self.

But this is only the case until it is not.

Everyone adopts, more or less, the culturally conditioned presumption that duality, or materialism, is real. That a separate subject and object fundamentally exist. That "*here* is me and *there* is everything else that is not me."

Yet at some point, be it right now, in a year, in twenty years, or when death seems near, we'll sense something different. No longer will we feel or recognize ourselves as separate. So, to a certain extent, we'll no longer be influenced by the belief in a separate self, separate world, separate material things, separate others, or a separate God.

In other words, when an apparently separate self turns the same knowing through which it knows objects inward, when it takes a sincere look at itself, when it inquires, "Who am I?"—limitations vanish and the true Self stands revealed. This inquiry is often prompted through the encouragement, guidance, or presence of a teacher or friend. It can also happen through a book or merely a quote. And, as I've put to you, it inspires further inquiries such as:

- Within whom or what do thoughts, feelings, sensations, and perceptions appear and disappear?
- Who is aware of thoughts, feelings, sensations, and perceptions?

- Can who I am be tarnished by thoughts, feelings, sensations, and perceptions?

Self-inquiry leads straight to the recognition that "I am not a limited object or separate self but rather the infinite and eternal knower and essence of all objects and selves." When this occurs, all objects and selves are divested of their apparent limitations too.

And the "practical" perk of this recognition?

The world is still a reflection. But not of separation, insecurity, or lack. Of equality, of love. Experience is now richly informed by the Being we share.

This is the purpose of this book. With the world outwardly divided, my hope is that we'll be guided inward toward Source's pathless path. That we'll wake up to who we truly are: infinite and eternal Consciousness. That we'll regard separate selves as mere objectifications of the only Self there is.

That, ultimately, we'll know no thing but the whole. No thing but peace. No thing but happiness. No thing but love.

THE CASE AGAINST ONENESS

Speaking of the whole, here's a significant question I wondered about early in my spiritual journey:

Why do many early spiritual teachers refer to the essence of experience, the essence of Being, as *non-duality* instead of *oneness*?

It turns out that there's an obvious reason, and another that's not so obvious.

Let's start with the obvious:

In sharing my work with audiences, when someone asks

about or uses the term *oneness*, it frequently implies "the act of becoming one." (Similar to how the term *forgetfulness* can imply "the act of becoming forgetful.") Because of this, the use of *oneness* potentially blurs the central theme of *True Self*: the Consciousness-only model. That is, the true Self, or Consciousness, never exists as two, so it can never become one. It's already non-dual (or not two). It's always whole, all that exists. And what is whole and all that exists can never become something else or connect to something else. There is no something else. Moreover, while I sometimes use *one* and *one with* as concessions (I'll discuss concessions at length in section 3), one is essentially "one too many." Consciousness has no edges or limits. It, as you know, is infinite.

Now for the not so obvious, which could be considered a continuation of the first reason:

To the separate selves we may still believe ourselves to be, experience is composed of concrete objects. But this distinct point of view is imagined or illusory. To the true Self, there are no concrete objects or distinctions. All appearances (separate objects) are made of the true Self. This is why those same spiritual teachers referenced at the outset of this note would say that "Consciousness knows only Consciousness" and "love knows everything as love," and why Jesus proclaimed, "I and my Father are one." As commonly used, then, *oneness* is just a flawed descriptor. If separation is illusory, the notion of two separate objects becoming one doesn't compute.

One last thing about the terms *non-duality* and *oneness* and their use:

While both terms represent reasonable attempts to capture

the indescribable essence of experience, the indivisible and mind-blowing nature of who we truly are, neither of them is perfect. Words never are. *Non-duality*, though, is the more accurate. Its use chips away at the confusion and burden of trying to establish a relationship with, or trying to connect to, what isn't separate to begin with: objects, others, etc.

Non-duality makes a bit more obvious the effortlessness and ease of Being.

BEFORE YOU TAKE THE PLUNGE

Rather than the aforementioned effortlessness and ease, do you sometimes experience struggle? Struggle is common; struggle is normal.

But . . .

Before you take the plunge into analyzing your thoughts, feelings, life situations, habits, relationships, mindset, or any object in order to cope with struggle, consider:

Is the substance of these objects different from the infinite and eternal space in which they appear and disappear?

If yes, take that plunge. If no, rather than analyze what appears and disappears, explore what objects are made of. Explore what always stays the same.

You get the gist.

Why explore what comes and goes?

Why explore the content rather than its substance?

Why explore what is not essential to you?

Why explore who or what you are not?

Explore you. Who are you?

Not thoughts and feelings, life situations, or any object.

They appear and disappear within Consciousness, are made of Consciousness, and are known by Consciousness too.

Are you struggling? (Or even if you're not.) Before you take the plunge into objects, explore the nature of Consciousness. Because Consciousness does not come and go. Because Consciousness is *you*.

LOVE, LACK, AND THE ESSENTIAL

At fifteen, my son Jackson was going through a breakup with his first girlfriend. Struggling, or innocently overlooking his true nature, he couldn't come to grips with losing someone who he thought was such an essential part of his life.

One day, in the midst of this struggle, I made my way up to his room, sat on his bed, and said, "I know you're upset, but remember, no one is essential to you."

With a bewildered look, Jackson asked, "Isn't Mommy essential to you? Don't you two need each other?"

I countered, "If something happened to your mother, I'd be crushed, but I'd endure. No, we don't need each other. And, believe it or not, this explains our strong marriage."

Jackson smiled and admitted, "I don't really get it, Dad, but for some reason it still makes sense."

"Perfect," I told him. "We'll revisit the subject later. Let's go outside, I'll hit you some ground balls." (He soon became a heck of a college ballplayer.)

"Awesome!"

And off we went.

Flash forward a decade. Both Jackson and I now "get it" much more clearly. While experiences come and experiences go, the true Self endures. It is permanent. Like a TV screen that stays the same no matter the changing of the channels, the true you cannot be altered.

As for why understanding the permanence of the true Self has implications for a strong and loving marriage:

We cannot be *in love* and, at the same time, *lack*. Love is the absence of lack, of all that is personal. Love has no wants, no needs; no push, no pull; no demands, no ego. Since love knows not of separation or transience, it makes no attempt to obtain something from or become secure through an "other." Love is the mutual recognition of the infinite and eternal Being we truly are.

For Jackson, for the rest of my family, and for you and your family—knowing this, and only this, is what's essential.

LET'S PAUSE FOR A BRIEF REMINDER

This far through *True Self*, you've likely recognized (as Jackson opened the door to seeing that day) that you're not an object or separate person yourself. As such, fulfillment can't be found in the world of objects. Only that which believes itself to be separate, to be limited and lacking, to not be infinite and eternal, would seek in that world.

This recognition is the most important of all. But, as a reminder, it can also be the most harrowing.

Once you've caught a glimpse of who you are and the fact that eternal peace is not found in the object-based world, you'll be more open, more sensitive, more vulnerable. Not less.

This is why not looking outward for distraction and relief is a massively courageous undertaking. You might find yourself returning to an old habit or object of desire, you might experience guilt, you might question if you have what it takes. It's all OK. Nothing is against the rules. Step by step, the sense of self that you've held on to for years is withering.

Yet I promise, although it might seem otherwise, this withering and the accompanying sense of loss and perhaps pain is appropriate. It's part of the deal, the journey. So, again, don't run. Please hang in there. No coping, beating yourself up, or quitting. You can't fill an illusory hole. The need for comfort is a lie.

Before a personal self, before belief, before a world of objects, home is where you long to be. You are the prodigal son or daughter. I am the same. And home is where we're heading right now.

THE JOURNEY HOME

Here are three more pointers, in the form of questions, about how things seem versus the reality of who or what we are:

- Why do we overlook that we are Consciousness itself rather than a transient image within Consciousness?
- Why do we forget that we are a singular Being and, instead, focus on the appearance of 7.5 billion separate or personal selves?
- Why is the world virtually consumed with, and hoodwinked by, the belief in separation, duality, or materialism?

There's a surprisingly simple answer to all of this. An answer that revolves around our journey of self-exploration and discovery, the "dissolution of belief and the knowing of Self" journey, the "I am not this for I am that" journey that tends to play out like this:

A baby is born. Consciousness (the baby's true nature) is merged, or one, with experience. The newborn has no understanding of separateness. It doesn't know itself as distinct from its mother, its cradle, or the room in which it sleeps. But because the baby's experience seems to be known from the perspective of a body, as the baby grows, it's perfectly normal for it to connect its identity to that body—the apparently finite point from which it seems to formulate experience. This, of course, is strictly confirmed by a culture that promotes the belief that the body is, without question, the experiencer; that the body is one and the same with who the baby truly is. Heck, this apparently finite point is even given a personal name.

As a result, at this "I am not my mother's body, I am *my* body" stage of the journey, the concept of being an individual, or a separate self, is solidified. And in spite of the inklings in the back of the mind that "there's more to me than this body and maybe I don't experience on behalf of or through a body," 99 percent of us pull the emergency brake on the journey right at this stage. Predictably, we live in a world that views separation as a fact, not as an appearance or illusion.

And who can blame us for halting this journey?

Those who question the existence of a separate self, who convey a knowing that "I am greater than this finite body," who express an interest in continuing the journey of self-exploration, almost always encounter pushback and societal resistance. Many are labeled as crazy, freakish, woo-woo, eccentric, or just plain-old weird. (Being a rugged athlete was my cover for years.)

What's more, virtually all self-help, religion, spirituality, and psychology experts cater to the idea of relieving the burden of the self. They promote self-belief, communication between selves, nurturing a soul, and other practices, tools, and techniques designed to fortify what one can never be: a secure separate entity.

Go back to the three versions of the inquiry at the top of this note. Do you know the answer now?

If not, there's this:

> *We live in a culture that has cut short the natural journey back to Source.*

This book, by contrast, was written to encourage you to bravely stay on this journey to who you truly are. My role, albeit provisional, is to remind you to not settle. To not allow our culture—and its mass of hardened, separate-seeming selves—to convince you that it's the only game in town. My role is to support the true Self.

Again and again, ask yourself:

- Who or what am I?
- Can a self, an "I" that is separate, be found?

- Can a separate object or world (separate from me, outside of me) be found?
- When I lose a sense of separation, lose the sense that "I am a body," what remains?
- Is there verifiable evidence that I experience on behalf of or through a body?
- Between thoughts, in deep sleep, and upon what we call death, where do I go?

No matter what a world of separate selves says, let's persevere on our journey inward.

KEEP QUESTIONING

Toward the end of a daylong meeting (my favorite way to teach/share) in early 2020, I was asked:

"If there's one message to take from today, Garret, what would it be?"

My answer:

"To understand that body-minds are not knowers; they are known. To realize that human beings don't have experiences; they are experienced. To, at the very least, question the primary belief that the one who knows or experiences is a separate self."

Now to accomplish all that, as you've probably caught on, one must be willing to hold still and investigate what part of a body and mind possesses the power to know or experience (or even the power to perceive or observe). And then to boldly admit that this part can't be found because this part doesn't exist.

You're still reading. I'm guessing you're willing. So, right here, let's examine if what I just said is true. Let's try to find a body part capable of knowing.

Is it the brain?

Well, I obviously get that this is what you've been taught. But how can a brain, an object, be aware or know? Where in the brain is this power? Even neurologists have yet to find the neural pathways that would make a brain aware (the "hard problem of consciousness" mentioned earlier).

How about the heart? The eyes?

How about the elbow, ears, wrist, or foot?

How about an electrical current or energy that runs through, charges, and informs all of these parts—kind of like a robot?

You get the idea.

Perhaps, rather than blindly follow the crowd and our culture, it finally makes good sense to question the primary belief.

And keep questioning. And question some more.

IT'S INTERESTING

When I question another offshoot of the primary belief, when I consider the possibility that we're not a multiplicity of beings—consider that I'm a singular Being, a singular Consciousness, with a "multiplicity" playing out within me—I still possess preferences or ideas of right and wrong. What I lose, however, is the tendency to blame the "others" that seem to make up this multiplicity when their preferences, behaviors, and ideas of right and wrong don't align with mine.

On the other hand, when I overlook this possibility, when I return to the old belief that I'm a separate part of a multiplicity—when I take myself to be a separate self—I'm tempted by and wrestle with the impulse to blame and lash out.

It's interesting.

BLAME

Once it becomes clear that rather than outside of the true Self, all of life appears within and is made of the true Self, we still (as just discussed) may not relish what appears within us. We may, for instance, take umbrage with someone's behavior. We may judge or criticize this behavior. But blame? Not so much. Because without the belief in separation, the belief that selves can somehow appear separate from or outside of us, there can't be a belief in personal responsibility or "doership." Or in blame.

Alas, due to our culture's widespread belief that experience *does* appear outside of us, that separation is true, that blame is appropriate, we're virtually incapable today of constructive debate. Interactions have turned personal. Hostility and vindictiveness run rampant. We argue to win and for someone else to lose, to add a notch to our belt, and not for the benefit of the greater good.

As a demonstration, let's say that one who's been conditioned to believe that he or she is a separate self (this obviously occurs in almost all cases), and so, too, believes that "others" are separate, faces criticism. No matter how sage the criticism might be, it will be taken personally—the very nature of the belief that "I am a separate person" *is* to take things personally. Plus, a war of words, or worse, will often ensue.

Scenarios like this even occur absent of direct criticism. How many times have you reacted angrily to a random social media post? It's not your fault. If you assume, as you've been taught to do, that experience takes place outside of you, that criticism comes from an "other," you will impulsively defend your turf. And as an aside, thinking that your reaction depends on the tone of the criticism is just more conditioning based on the lie of separation. As with all experience, tone takes place within you too.

Perhaps, then, it's blame—not judgment or criticism—that ails us. And blame, including our debilitating habit of self-blame, results from our cultural belief in a duality that doesn't exist. All objects and others are made of Consciousness. That's all there is. From the perspective of purity, of truth, there's nothing to blame and there's no one to blame.

One more thing: No worries if you look within and still see separation. No trouble if your emotions stir. (Conditioning is stubborn.) If you don't believe in the separation or duality you see, however, blame is history. Conflict too.

A MATTER OF HARMONY

The umbrella term for the seemingly separate physical substances you see, or sense, is *matter*. Matter, according to most, is what all things are made of. "I'm made of matter, and other people, objects, and animals are also made of matter" is one scientific explanation for the apparent separation between me and everything else that is "not me."

But there's an issue with this belief about separation and matter: Nothing *can* exist separate from or outside of me, the whole. So while scientists keep trying, just as they can't find the localization of Consciousness inside a body, they've yet to find this "physical substance" called matter. Seriously. Go ahead and do an online search for "Does matter exist?" You'll be amazed at what comes up.

Rather than continuing to seek this physical substance called matter, then, perhaps it's time for scientists and the rest of us to admit that there's a good chance that matter doesn't exist. (Or, at a minimum, it doesn't exist as we think it does.) Perhaps we should consider what's staring us right in the face—that all things are made of Consciousness. Perhaps when we realize that Consciousness is all there is, the "not me" of materialism will be replaced with "we are not two." Perhaps then we'll experience harmony.

Here's a metaphor pertaining to the nonexistence of matter that I learned from a terrific teacher of the Consciousness-only model, Francis Lucille:

Imagine you're on a video call with two of your friends. What you experience on your phone or computer screen is three separate boxes with three separate faces. You appear to see what is "me" (made of matter) and what is "not me" (made of matter). You observe lines of distinction. But take a closer look. Even tap on the screen. What are the boxes, faces, and lines of distinction really made of?

The answer: the screen. Or you could say that all things are the screen. And the screen is a metaphor for the nature of all things, Consciousness. By accepting separation as real or true, we've completely overlooked that separate objects exist in appearance only. They're not made of matter. Try again to find them. What you'll find is Consciousness.

Accomplished scientists have researched, analyzed, and experimented. They've tried to substantiate the apparent separation between "me" and everything else. They've tried to clarify the distinction between a perceiving subject and a perceived object. They've tried to find separate things made of matter. They've tried to prove duality.

All to no avail.

That's why it's only by recognizing the illusory nature of separation—recognizing that everything is an image of Consciousness, appearing within Consciousness, made of Consciousness—that harmony in your family, community, country, or the world will be found.

WHAT CAN'T BE IMPROVED

Yet, still, we seek harmony by trying to improve not only our relationships, but also by trying to improve our thoughts, feelings, and states of mind.

Here's a concise reminder as to why this is always a struggle:

Thoughts, feelings, and states don't arise within a body. They arise within the true Self, within you, within infinite and eternal Consciousness.

Thoughts, feelings, and states can't be improved.

They're made of what's infinite and eternal too.

THE EMPTY AFTERMATH

Have you ever worked hard toward an end goal and reached it, only to be left with an empty feeling afterward? It's more common than you might think.

Over the years, I've had numerous discussions with those who couldn't make heads or tails of this dilemma. They've succeeded, achieved what they've dreamed of since childhood, so why would they now describe their feeling-state as empty or, in some cases, miserable?

It all starts with intention. These "hard workers" have spent the better part of their lives seeking an object when the only true intention or desire is causeless joy, the knowing of their own Being. (More on this topic shortly in "The Only Desire," p. 164.)

An athlete who strives relentlessly for a championship, for instance, doesn't truly desire a championship, an object. So, in the aftermath of winning, he or she is left empty. The pull toward Source has not been satisfied. Sadly, most don't realize what just took place. They believe their emptiness is a sign to restart the search for objects—and the cycle continues.

Until, that is, it doesn't.

Sometimes after a tragic event, sometimes after asking a teacher of true nature a question, sometimes while walking in nature with a friend, or sometimes for no apparent reason, we wake up to the truth: Well-being cannot be found in the material world.

I'm not saying championships aren't cool, mind you. I'm saying that as an expression of self-exploration and upon the discovery of the true Self, championships stop being the aim. Source is. Peace is. Love is. As is Happiness.

No matter your career or interests, what could be more freeing?

Let's go play.

MY CONFUSION

Odds are that you now appreciate, more than just a little, the fallacy of seeking in the material world. Odds are that it's become clear that identifying with objects, or trying to find comfort in them, equates to turning your back on Source. Turning your back on answers. Turning your back on peace, on love, on happiness.

But I still want to be super certain that you're not overlooking a big piece to this puzzle.

Namely, that the conventional cognitive approach (used by counselors, coaches, and self-help professionals) of delving into your thoughts—trying to understand, analyze, or improve them—is also turning your back on Source. Thoughts, again, are objects. Like other objects, they appear and disappear. Like other objects, they are known. Pointing toward objects, or yearning for an upgraded variety of them, is the opposite of pointing toward Source.

Why do I bring up this topic and nuanced description at this stage of this book?

Simple. When I realized where my own confusion was coming from (I was trying to step away from Source, or who I am, in an attempt to find who I am), when I awoke to the absurdity in placing importance on thoughts, my life and my work changed on a dime.

See if your experience matches mine.

The ego seeks answers in thoughts and other objects.

The true Self never wanders.

STAY WITH THE FEELING

Feelings, of course, are objects too.

Like trying to manage thoughts, trying to push discomfort or anxiety away, trying to cope or manage feelings, elicits confusion. It narrows focus and heightens tension. It reinforces the belief that the essence of each feeling is different. It upholds the subsequent belief that certain feelings are unbearable.

Rather, before you attempt to cope, *wait*. Stay with the feeling. Bring it close. So close that you can't tell the difference between yourself and the feeling.

You just might find, in your actual experience, that nothing is unbearable (or even harmful). The true Self is open, lovingly impartial. You are both one with and free from whatever arises within.

NO ONE IS BROKEN

"No one is broken."

How often have you come across this refrain or belief? I have a lot. And yet, rather than automatically accept this refrain as true and share it, here's more self-inquiry:

Who is this "one" that is not and cannot be broken?

Is it the true Self to which I just referred, or the separate self from which I was pointing away?

Without clarification, confusion is a pretty sure bet. Because an individual, personal, or separate you is indeed broken. Or, more aptly described: divided, insecure, not even a thing. "I am a separate self" is an idea, a transient modulation within and made of who you truly are: the eternal Being—Consciousness—that is indivisible and, yes, cannot be broken.

So skip trying to convince a separate self that it's not broken (or that it's resilient). That's like trying to teach a shadow to walk.

"You are broken." "You are not broken." Who or what is being addressed?

Call the separate self out for precisely what it is: a transient idea or modulation that yearns to be whole. And then point to the wholeness in which this idea or modulation arises.

No *one* is broken.

Right on.

The true Self can never be split.

STUCK IN YOUR OWN ADVICE

The next time you're about to suggest yet another common refrain, that someone seek such objects as success, greatness, an enhanced personal image, a secure relationship, or becoming more complete—take a breather, a step back if you will, and ask yourself:

- Am I the one who's seeking?
- Am I the one who's overlooking my true nature, overlooking that the true Self is already complete?

- Am I the one who's yearning to hold still, simply be, and allow life to take care of itself?

Remember: Seeking an object is what gives rise to confusion, and to suffering. It can only be *you* who's stuck in the suffering of your own advice.

ALWAYS CONSCIOUSNESS, ONLY CONSCIOUSNESS

This "you" to which I just referred, this you who overlooks the essence of its own Being, highlights an often missed but essential aspect of self-exploration or returning home to Source:

> *This "you" is not a person.*

No person is capable of veiling, overlooking, or forgetting the nature of Self. No person is capable of unveiling, waking up, or remembering.

Only Consciousness, so to speak, is capable.

I know. Your conditioning is stubborn. So, for a second, let's placate the belief that you are indeed a separate person or self. Let's go with the belief in personal control.

I now ask:

- Why would you choose to overlook your very own essence?
- Why would you choose to be separate?

- What part of you provides the power of forgetting, remembering, choosing, or being in control? Where is this power found?

You'll search and search for the answers.

Veiling and unveiling, the appearance of duality and the dissolution of this appearance: These are not the workings of a human being. They're the natural properties of Consciousness. The belief that human beings are personally accountable for the forgetting (or remembering) of who or what they truly are, when you get right down to it, is nonsensical.

For example, as my colleague and editor Joel Drazner likes to tell:

Clark Kent gets nervous and makes mistakes, he gets insecure as he romances Lois Lane, he gets frustrated with his boss, Perry White. But wait a minute. Who really gets caught up in all of that? Is it Clark Kent or is it Superman?

It's Superman. Clark Kent, a disguise, can't get caught up in something.

And who or what, relative to this example, forgets who you truly are?

It's Consciousness. How can a modulation within Consciousness, a human being, possibly forget?

It's Consciousness that seems to get lost in a world within itself.

It's Consciousness that seems to veil its infinite and eternal nature and overlook that a veil is in place.

It's Consciousness (which is never truly asleep) that seems to wake up to the nature of experience, to the fact that all things are illusory.

Always Consciousness. Only Consciousness.

It's never, ever personal.

SEEKING A FEELING

Something else to not overlook—that a feeling of security, calm, clarity, positivity, or even bliss does not signify a return to true nature.

A "good feeling" is not who you are. It's not your true nature.

Feelings arise and dissolve within you. Feelings are made of you. You, however, are not made of them.

You, again, are not a feeling.

You don't feel a feeling.

There's no use seeking a feeling.

You stay the same, regardless of any feeling.

Keep your attention on the whole, the unchangeable space in which all objects, including feelings, arise and dissolve without resistance.

Keep your attention on Consciousness, on Source.

Keep your attention on you.

EINSTEIN'S TAKE ON TRUTH AND EXPERIENCE

Perhaps when Einstein said, "Truth is what stands the test of experience," he didn't mean the personal *content* of experience (the various occurrences in one's so-called "life," the objects and situations that arise and dissolve, the thoughts and feelings that come and go).

Perhaps he was prodding us to explore the *nature* of experience, toward this recognizable inquiry:

Can an object, person, situation, thought, or feeling appear separate from experience?

Asked differently:

Without the power to experience, would anything exist? Is duality true? Do the objects of experience exist separate from or outside of you? Aren't all objects made of the exact same stuff?

Perhaps Einstein wanted us to explore the foundation of peace, love, and happiness; to explore what never changes, what's always present, and that which is infinite and eternal.

Not a separate self. Not separate objects.

But the true Self, indeed.

WHAT IT TAKES

It's not unusual for me to hear or read some version of the following objection to my work:

> But Garret, it will take years to understand who I truly am; years to grasp the intimacy of all experience; years to be able to clearly explain true nature, Consciousness, or non-duality to my clients, audiences, or family. I have to teach, coach, parent, or be a friend. I have to make a living. I have to live my life!

Fair enough. It could take years. So an idea:

Live life from right where you are, as you are. Share with the world what you know.

But one caveat:

Make sure that how you live and what you share point to the knower, not the known. To Source, rather than away from it. To what experience reveals, as opposed to our culturally conditioned beliefs.

For example, suggesting that someone visualize success, the flight of a golf ball, or a million dollars in the bank is not the same as suggesting that someone visualize who they were prior to the indoctrination of conditioning. Suggesting that someone explore thoughts and feelings is not the same as suggesting that someone explore the space in which thoughts and feelings arise and dissolve. Suggesting that someone look within the body and mind for answers is not the same as suggesting that someone look within the Self.

It's basic.

For a life of giving and sharing, for a life of genuine expression, of love, all it takes is resolutely pointing inward.

And you have what it takes.

Because you, my friend, *are* what it takes.

BANISH A THOUGHT, BANISH A FEELING

Back to thoughts and feelings, the most easily misunderstood of objects. Have you ever banished, or discarded, them?

What I mean is: Have you ever applied a self-help or mind

strategy of some kind, and, as a result, observed a thought or feeling leaving you?

Then why keep trying?

An object can't leave the whole.

All thoughts and feelings are modulations within you, made of you. You can't rid you of you.

You are the whole. You are the universe. You are Consciousness.

Instead of trying to rid yourself of certain thoughts and feelings in order to fulfill some materialistic desire—why else would you try such a thing?—perhaps knowing who you are is all that you truly long for.

LEAVE THEM ALONE

I suppose the opposite of trying to banish something would be to simply live with that something. And if you're a teacher, coach, counselor, or advice-giver of some kind, I'm going to ask you to consider advising your clients to do just that—to live with the "somethings." But especially with their *thoughts* and *feelings*.

Because while techniques to manage, resist, or seek better versions of these somethings, these thoughts and feelings, might have been part of your training, such techniques are effectively useless. Those consumed by the belief that "I am a separate self" will resist, seek, and *suffer* nevertheless (that's what a separate self does). You're better off staying away from the belief in personal thinking and feelings or *any* methodology that places them front and center. You're better off avoiding the endorsement of "having less on your mind" or the theoretical benefit of "gaining inner calm."

Preferably, guide the sufferer back to the infinite and eternal space in which thoughts and feelings are free to do as they please. To that which is open, welcoming, and knows nothing of preference. To the true Self that remains unmoved, whole, and present regardless of the objects that arise and dissolve within.

One's relationship with thoughts and feelings will then, with ease, take care of itself.

HOW FAR WE'VE STRAYED

How far from reality we've strayed. In our culture and lexicon today . . .

- "I am finite and limited" is normal. "I am infinite and eternal" is eccentric.
- "I am an individual" is normal. "We are one Being" is eccentric.
- "A body is conscious" is normal. "A body is an image within Consciousness" is eccentric.
- "A body (or brain) has or contains thoughts" is normal. "A body is a thought (an idea)" is eccentric.
- "A body has experiences" is normal. "A body is experienced" is eccentric.
- "You were born and will die" is normal. "You are the eternal space in which all things are born and die" is eccentric.

- "Come together" is normal. "We're not separate" is eccentric.
- "Believe" is normal. "Look to experience" is eccentric.
- "Be positive" is normal. "Welcome all thoughts and feelings" is eccentric.
- "Find your purpose" is normal. "Explore who you are" is eccentric.
- "Personal control, responsibility, burden (and blame)" are normal. "An absence of burden (and an absence of blame)" is eccentric.
- "Seeking greatness" is normal. "The true Self is ordinary, standard, basic" is eccentric.
- "Love is found in a person" is normal. "Love is revealed upon the dissolution of the personal" is eccentric.
- "Beauty is found in objects" is normal. "Beauty is revealed upon the dissolution of objects" is eccentric.
- "Doing research or pursuing data-driven evidence" is normal. "Self-inquiry" is eccentric.
- "Investigating how objects interact (cause-and-effect)" is normal. "Investigating the very nature of objects (what objects are made of)" is eccentric.
- "Curing symptoms or problem-solving" is normal. "Getting to the primary root of problems (the belief that 'I am a separate self')" is eccentric.

- "Love as a unification strategy" is normal. "Love as our very essence" is eccentric.
- "All experiences take place outside of me, separate from me" is normal. "All experiences take place within me, made of me" is eccentric.

I could carry on, but let's just end with this:

> *What appears real is unreal. What appears unreal is real.*

Our starting point is incorrect.
Not human beings; we are a singular Being, one Consciousness.
How far we've strayed.

THE HEART OF RESILIENCE

This, in some form or another, is the question I've been asked most often over the course of my career:

"How can I handle both physical and emotional pain with more ease?"

Sometimes this question is asked within the context of mental toughness: "Why are some people so gritty, durable, stalwart, or tough?"

Experience reveals, though, that sifting through materialistic ideas like "grittiness" or "toughness" clouds the answer. It's but another example of how far we've strayed, as toughness brings fleeting results at best. And if you've ever tried to will yourself through pain, you know the fallacy in that.

What, then, lies at the heart of resilience?

Consider this:

Resilience is the effect of a deep knowing that pain, rather than being located within the body, is nothing more than a modulation within the true Self, the whole we call Consciousness.

This is why animals handle injury or bumps and bruises with ease. They don't identify themselves as the body—how would they know to do that? Pain appears. But it's not personalized. It belongs to the whole (Consciousness) and is fluidly absorbed into the whole. Consciousness, too, has no problem with pain. All things that modulate or appear within Consciousness, including injury or physical and emotional pain, are made of itself.

The bottom line is that those who believe the true Self is equivalent to the body, or that they truly are the body, will grab on to pain, feel pain, own pain, complain about pain, be influenced by pain, suffer from pain, and ultimately attempt to will themselves *through* pain. Mental-toughness techniques, substances, excursions, constant visits to gurus, and "spiritual" practices such as yoga or meditation are the most common of vehicles.

And while this note is not meant to suggest that the experience of pain should be ignored, or that efforts to get to its root, heal from sickness, or get fit and trim are unwise, it does provide an uncommon direction regarding the heart of resilience.

Pain, whether physical or emotional, need not be countered or conquered.

The heart of resilience is the knowing of our own Being. That we're one with all things. That no matter what arises within, we are perpetually well.

NON-DUALITY, NON-DUALISM

A clarification:

- Non-duality = all existing things are made of our own Being, or Consciousness. Consciousness is all that exists.
- Non-dualism = nothing exists.

True Self was written to help reveal the non-dual essence of all things. It was not written to promote non-dualism.

So in response to the frequent outrage stemming from the confusion between non-duality and non-dualism—"Garret, how can you claim that humans don't exist?"—*yes*, humans, or people, do exist.

But as experience reveals, they do not exist separate from or outside of you. They exist as appearances (or illusions) within you. All things do.

The question, of course, then becomes: Who are you?

Can the one in which all things exist be a person?

Exactly.

The true Self = Consciousness.

And not only do people exist, or appear, within you, they're made of you too.

SIMPLY BE

Are you doing your best to "simply be"?

It's difficult, yes?

That's because this often-advised task, this zen-sounding strategy for soothing pain and discomfort, is also born from confusion. The confusion of mistaken identity, or "Who am I?"

Another idea, one that I often advise, would be to cease *trying* to chill, meditate, or simply be (for a materialistic purpose) and answer this version of our essential question:

Does life appear outside of you or within you?

If life appears outside of you, then all things are separate from you.

If life appears within you, then all things are one with you, made of you.

Our culture, as you know, has presumed and then accepted the former, that life appears outside of you or us, to be true. So—and see if this aligns with your experience—we seek both self-preservation and connection. We're consumed by the belief in separation, by the desire to stand on our own two feet. Yet we also intuit a deeper unity. We feel pushed and pulled in opposing directions. We fail to reach either. Confusion reigns. Behaviors become questionable. We can't simply be.

But what if rather than the need for behavioral fixes (rules, laws, strategies, therapies), our confusion merely signifies that our cultural presumption is backward? As I've proposed, what if the latter—that life appears within us—is true?

Would we seek self-preservation? Connection?

Don't think so. Knowing that all things are one with us (and, again, see if this aligns for you), we'd have no cause to seek.

That's the reason I'm going to keep encouraging you to set your sights solely on our essential question.

If life appears outside of you, you'll constantly seek. The push and pull, the confusion between self-preservation and connection, will continue.

If life appears within you, there's nothing to seek. You won't be pushed and pulled. All things, made of the same essence, freely arise and dissolve. You will *simply be*.

NO GIFT OF LIFE

Remaining on the topic of life, I've been told that I once received "the gift" of it.

But did I?

Here's what I know *for sure*:

I witness, or experience, life. A life filled with things—people, animals, places, and events. But I don't witness myself, the one who witnesses, in that life.

I witness life. But I have no evidence that this life is witnessed by a person named Garret.

I witness life. But I have not witnessed receiving the "gift of life." I have never appeared. I have not witnessed myself being born.

I witness life. But I have not witnessed the one (a higher power or God) who supposedly gave me the "gift of life."

I witness life. But, again, I am not an object in this life.

I witness life. All of life appears and disappears within me.

I witness life. But life is not personal. Out of me, Consciousness, all of life is made.

VEILING AND UNVEILING

The objects of experience vary, as they always will.

You may, for instance, come across a closed-minded and intolerant person. Then, soon after, an open-minded and hospitable person.

But here's something on which to keep reflecting:

What you're always experiencing is the veiling and unveiling, or the forgetting and remembering, of yourself, Consciousness. As a result of this veiling and unveiling, people and things of apparently different "quality" will come and go constantly.

You may disapprove of or appreciate such people and things. You may sometimes get stern with them; you may sometimes get tender. Either way, you're always experiencing the transient nature of the objects *within* yourself brought about by the veiling and unveiling *of* yourself.

As I explained in "Blame" (p. 142), don't fault the objects. They're all manifestations of Consciousness.

INSECURITY AND ATTACHMENT

Those with whom I work will almost always bring up the "dreaded" sensation of insecurity. They'll claim to be insecure about this or that object or situation. They'll seek to end this apparently detrimental experience. They'll assume that part of my role is to help them cope, to help them find their way out of it.

Well, my role has never been that, not in the slightest. It's actually the opposite. It's to remind them that insecurity, as with any glaring or over-the-top experience, is the effect of one thing:

attaching their identity or well-being to any object or situation. (Again, I'm defining an object as anything that is known.) Insecurity is *supposed* to result when we identify with objects. It's a sign that the veil is in place. It's natural and appropriate. Objects come and go. They are transient. The veil comes and goes. It is transient. We are not.

By way of analogy, many of us have experienced insecurity or the sensation of being out of sorts as we've lived through the trials and tribulations of our chosen career. But this experience doesn't arise because of our career, an object. It arises when we try to attach who we are, our identity or sense of self, to who we aren't: our career, an object.

Fortunately, once we understand where insecurity is coming from and what it's telling us, an intuitive solution tends to appear. Specifically this:

As it makes less and less sense to attach our well-being to something that evolves, changes, appears, or disappears, we now turn our attention toward what always remains the same. Toward what's perpetually dependable and unfailing. Toward the permanent.

And with this return to who we truly are, Consciousness, the experiences within us—whether bad, good, or indifferent—increasingly lose their grip.

THE ONLY DESIRE

The turning of intention toward the permanent unveils another crucial aspect of our journey home—that there is only *one desire*.

Yet, to digress, this desire is first veiled in personal quests, such as:

- Success
- Fame
- Fortune
- Relationships
- Security
- Positivity
- Clarity of mind

Or even in noble and global quests, such as:

- Saving the environment
- The alleviation of suffering
- Protesting for equal rights
- Eliminating famine

Trouble is, these quests aren't working. What we seek remains elusive. What we attempt to fix persists in droves.

What are we missing?

Just the theme of this book. We're seeking objects, and seeking solace in objects, when the only true desire is the knowing of our own Being—happiness, causeless joy. We're spinning our wheels. We're bolstering the sense of lack that our quests are attempting to fix.

Still think this may be the case for me, but not for you?

Take this quick quiz and find out.

You can have either (not both):

a. The apparent object of your desire—the relationship, the reward, the fortune

b. Happiness

If you're honest, you'll select *b*, always *b*, since happiness underlies all desires.

So, then, why not cut out the middleman completely? Why not cease seeking objects and go directly at the only desire? Why not stop adding to the confusion and tumult, hold still, and explore directly inward?

You just might find that the knowing of your own Being, the knowing of happiness, will be your greatest gift to the world.

A WORLD OF ONE

As we make our way to section 3, I now submit, with a tinge of frustration about the state of the world, the obvious:

> *Provided the primary belief, "I am a separate self," remains intact, we won't know happiness (or peace, or love).*

It's also obvious that at the core of every calamity or misfortune the world has ever known is the belief, the lie, that a separate self is the one who experiences. That "separation" is real. And steeped in such a belief, we can resist injustice, look to research and science for answers, try our best to communicate and connect, pursue relief in states of mind or materialistic success, study an endless supply of strategies and theories, even pray to God—but because we're living a lie, we're stuck. The lie of separation has us dazed, confused, and incapable of harmony. We keep going deeper and deeper into the lie in order to find a cure for the isolation and suffering that the lie has wrought.

Even teachers, coaches, counselors, consultants, writers, and speakers whose careers are based on helping others out of confusion are perpetuating the lie. In order to help a separate self out of confusion, the existence of separation must be validated. Yet validating the existence of separation is the catalyst of confusion. And suffering. And conflict. And violence. And on and on.

Here in the United States, for example, one cure for these ills gaining steam is to place mental health counselors in every school and organization, on every team, on every street corner, it seems. These counselors have also been trained to believe the lie. They're taught to secure what can't be secured—the psyche or separate self. See where I'm heading? This is the opposite of a solution. This is the lie perpetuating the lie.

The same can be said of these materialistic quests: shoring up borders, demonstrating military prowess, mandating health policies, and retreating into groups, ethnicities, political parties, nations, or religions. Not to mention the ploy of promoting diversity (the illusion of separation) under the auspices of advancement. We're even prejudiced against the prejudiced right now. For goodness' sake, we're waging war on ourselves.

How the heck did we get here?

To be fair, appearances are deceiving. Our culture is essentially built on the one thing—"I am a separate self living in a world of separate objects"—that, while it appears real, has never been experienced. And it essentially discards the one thing—"I am the whole, I am Consciousness itself"—that, while it appears unreal, has *always* been experienced.

I ask again, have you ever experienced the absence of Consciousness?

Of course not. (And if you're possibly curious about the sense of absence during deep sleep or while under anesthesia, how would this absence be known if Consciousness weren't there?)

Have you ever experienced the absence of the body or self?

Of course. (And if you're questioning this claim, think again about deep sleep or being under anesthesia when you have no sense that you're a body or a self living in a world.)

Consciousness (you) has always been present. Bodies appear and disappear, and the world does too, but you do not. All things are one with you, made of you, known by you. There's no such thing as separation. And while even at this stage separation's nonexistence (including and especially "you" as a concrete separate self) might seem a bit nebulous, if you keep exploring the genuine nature of experience—and at all costs are prepared to question your closely held beliefs—who you are *will* become clear.

It will also become clear that, other than no longer seeking your identity in objects, no deliberate action is required to eradicate the belief in separation and the isolation and insecurity provoked by it. We don't need to try to come together as one. We don't need motivational speeches, team-building exercises, or charismatic preachers suggesting the methods through which to love one another or unite. These are examples of the "stuckness," the wheel-spinning, I mentioned before. What is not two cannot unite. What is whole need not come together. Merely recognizing separation as a belief is what demolishes this belief, bringing down the house of cards and the artificiality that dictates our lives that teeters on top of it.

Needless to say, please don't believe a word I've written in this note or on any page of this book. Not one. As usual, check in with your own experience.

Do you know for certain that without you, an other or any object even exists? Can anything appear outside of the whole or apart from you? Do you truly witness on behalf of or through a body? Is separation true? Explore for yourself. If the exploration becomes too daunting, then feel free to check in with me. As we've gone over, the ego—the product of the belief in separation, a transient image or illusion within you, Consciousness—will fight hard for its apparent existence. The ego will resist. The one thing it can't stand is to be seen for what it really is.

But we are ready. Our number's been called. With unwavering love and support, this is the time and place to rigorously explore who and what we are. To thirst for truth. To take a courageous look within and uncover what's actually going on.

The primary belief has finally met its match. While the appearance will linger, the belief in separation cannot.

A world of peace—a world of one—is so within reach.

It is here. It is now.

Section 3, "True Self in the World," awaits.

INQUIRIES AND ANSWERS

How do I know for sure that I am Consciousness, not a body?

To be something, you'd have to experience the presence of that something 24/7. What's the one "thing" you always experience? Not a body. That one thing, who or what you are, is Consciousness.

When the belief in separation dies, why does the appearance of separation remain?

Conditioning. We're taught to believe that we're separate beings. We're taught to see and label objects as separate or distinct. When it becomes evident that we're not separate beings but one Being, the appearance of separation remains seared into experience. It's just now seen for the illusion it's been all along.

In teaching or coaching, we often hear that it's imperative to meet people where they are (at their own level of understanding). How does that make sense from the perspective of Consciousness?

It doesn't. While you can answer a question at the level of the question, don't waste a second analyzing a person's level of understanding. You'll analyze for the foreseeable future. Know yourself. Know that all others share your Being. Where others are is where you are. All interactions will be informed by this knowing.

Distressing thoughts and feelings sometimes weigh on me like a boulder. What should I do?

Bring the boulder close. So close that you can't tell the difference between you and it.

The boulder is not oppressive. What's oppressive is trying to push it away or resist it. Doing so distances you from the recognition that thoughts and feelings are made of Consciousness, of love. Thoughts and feelings are made of you.

What do you mean by "Ignorance is shared"?

Let's say you experience someone doing or saying something that you deem ignorant. Within what does that person appear? Out of what is that person made? The answers are: you and you. That person's ignorance cannot appear separate from or outside of you. So it's "shared." *Ignorance* is simply another word for the veiling, or the ignoring, of the true Self.

Am I guided by Consciousness?

You are not. But this common belief is important to examine.

Are you separate from Consciousness? No. How can anything be separate from or appear outside of Consciousness? And if you're not separate from Consciousness, then it's impossible for you to be guided by Consciousness—you *are* Consciousness.

Where does my unhappiness come from, and why does it arise?

Unhappiness arises when the unattainable goal of personal happiness is sought. More significant, don't make the common mistake of thinking that unhappiness and happiness are antonyms. Unhappiness is a transient feeling. Happiness, regardless of feelings, is who you are.

The way I see it, the game of life is to understand that each soul, with its own experiences, is a branch of a single Consciousness. Make sense?

As an allowance or concession, maybe. But, as you point out, Consciousness is singular. So better to not divide it or give credence to the belief that we're separate "souls."

There are not 7.5 billion representations of Consciousness, each having their own individual experiences. There is one Consciousness, one true Self, and the entirety of experience is appearing within it right now.

You sometimes seem critical of teachings or methods. Is it helpful to be critical?

I sometimes criticize. I never blame. That said, criticism absent of blame can indeed be helpful. It can sharpen us, rectify misunderstanding, and chip away at the shared veil of ignorance. Without criticism, experts and authorities remain unchecked and personal viewpoints spread unfiltered. As we've experienced throughout history, this is extremely dangerous. It puts certain human beings on pedestals. It births religious dogma and divide-and-conquer mentalities.

From the perspective of the true Self, criticism is impersonal and welcomed. All criticism holds a hint of truth.

Why do I vacillate between seeing and not seeing? Between calm and crisis? Between knowing and forgetting that I'm not separate?

It seems that way, but you don't truly vacillate as you describe. This is a misinterpretation based on the conditioned and erroneous belief that objects (material things, thoughts, feelings, sensations, perceptions—all of which come and go) are made of something other than Consciousness.

Consciousness is all there is. In fact, the idea that you vacillate is itself an object that's made of Consciousness.

I've heard you mention that self-exploration obliterates the separate self or ego. But you've also mentioned that the ego is illusory. How do you square these two statements?

Separation is an illusion. No object has appeared, or could appear, separate from or outside of the whole. So a separate or personal self is an illusion too. As is what I would term *ego*, the derivative of the belief that experience occurs from a personal perspective.

Self-exploration, to square my statements as you asked, is the process of first eliminating the belief that the separation we see is real (like eliminating the belief that the "water" in a desert mirage is real water), then doing the same to the belief that what we see, or experience, occurs on behalf of or through a person or separate self.

Managing, resisting, or trying to push bad thoughts and feelings away, in my experience, certainly perpetuates them. But why is this the case?

While my main suggestion is to trust the experience that you just described, this short explanation might be helpful too: Because no object, including thoughts and feelings, can arise anywhere but within you, no object can be separated from you. That's why resisting or trying to separate yourself from thoughts and feelings is an impossible and perpetually confounding task.

What's more, thoughts and feelings that can only arise within you must be made of you. And who are you? Consciousness, or love, itself. Can you imagine that you've been resisting love?

Do you have a take on goal setting?

My take is that the only true goal or desire is happiness, the knowing of our infinite and eternal Self. It's cool to set some object-based goals. It would be a mistake, though, to seek happiness in or through them.

What's the difference between non-duality and therapeutic modalities such as CBT (cognitive behavioral therapy) and NLP (neuro-linguistic programming)? Why do most counselors or therapists seem to push back on non-duality?

Therapeutic modalities are used to temporarily comfort "separate" people. Non-duality is a description of the singular essence or reality of all things, including the appearance of separate people.

Counselors tend to push back on non-duality out of fear that it will render their work obsolete. But this is a misunderstanding. The true Self doesn't render anything obsolete. Fact is, I know a handful of wonderful counselors who explore non-duality with vigor.

In a peculiar way, you don't always answer the question you're being asked. But you somehow get to the answer. What's up with that?

I suppose what's up is that I first explore the presumptions, the beliefs, that underlie a question before weighing the question's content. A how-do-I-do-something question, for example, is based on the presumption that "I am the doer." So first, I would address that presumption. The answer to the question will then spontaneously flow.

Never experiencing the absence or disappearance of Awareness (or Consciousness) doesn't seem accurate to me. What am I missing if I sometimes feel spaced out, if I sometimes fall into deep sleep and black out at night, or if I sometimes have no awareness of time?

Nothing. You've just been trained to take Awareness as a property of the body. From this conditioned perspective, while Awareness seems to disappear, it's actually the body, or the belief that "I am a body," that's disappearing.

You brought up deep sleep. Absent from deep sleep are objects—thoughts, dreams, the belief that "I am the body." But who or what is aware of this absence? Not the body. In deep sleep, any sense that "I am the body" is gone.

Let's now rephrase your initial comment. Not only have we never experienced the absence or disappearance of Awareness, we've also never experienced either the gradual or instantaneous appearance of Awareness. While objects appear and disappear, Awareness is always present. And what's always present cannot experience the appearance or disappearance of itself.

Last but not least: If Awareness is always present, and this ever-presence applies only to Awareness, then Awareness (or Consciousness) must be who or what we truly are.

My tendency to judge is terrible. How can I break free from this habit?

All likes and dislikes arise and dissolve within you. The totality of experience cannot be found anywhere else. Judgments, consequently, are made of you. And from you, they cannot be removed or separated.

You've been led to believe that judgments or preferences are wrong and that they're your fault. This isn't true, and acting on mistruth—in this case, seeking to not be judgmental—brings confusion and suffering.

Who is the one with preferences? Who are you? When you establish that all judgments or preferences belong to the whole, belong to Consciousness, they will fluidly arise and dissolve, free from burden.

A guy at work is being so difficult right now. I'm taking a stand as Consciousness and befriending him, but he's getting more and more disrespectful. Should I just let him be?

Consciousness doesn't befriend. Consciousness doesn't let be. Nor does Consciousness push away. Taking a stand as Consciousness simply means to recognize that no one exists separate from or outside of you; that you are always experiencing the inside of yourself; that regardless of their behavior, everyone shares your Being. Taking a stand, then, requires no strategic outreach on your part. It's simply being in the world knowingly as yourself.

As far as the guy at work, look at him from this non-dual perspective and let's see what happens to his disrespect.

Why do your posts and videos present an opposite position from the norm? It's as if you disagree or compete with every other expert.

That's funny. I don't view my posts and videos as disagreeing or competing. Even when I played and coached ice hockey, competition was nothing more than earnest cooperation to me. Today, I scrutinize direct experience and ask you to do the same. We then compare, contrast, debate, "compete"—until satisfied. Like I intimated, competition is cooperation in disguise.

I've witnessed the birth of my kids. I've witnessed my parents dying. How in the world can you say that me being born and dying are beliefs?

Your question, and perhaps simmering outrage, is understandable. It reveals the extent that our beliefs are so deeply rooted that we can't tell the difference between them and what's true. On this account, here, we stick to our direct experience. Only direct experience will reveal truth.

You have experienced the birth of your kids and the passing of your parents. But you, the knower of all events—Consciousness, Awareness—have never experienced yourself being born or dying. You've never experienced the appearance or disappearance of yourself.

If you stick with direct experience, you'll find that images, thoughts, feelings, sensations, and perceptions come and go within you. You are constant.

"Focus on my own experience rather than belief." OK, but what about my wife's experience that's happening a thousand miles from here? Are you saying that her experience shouldn't be relevant to me?

Experience is relevant. Conditioned beliefs for which you have no explicit evidence, such as your wife having her own experience a thousand miles away, are not.

Here's what I mean: Direct experience indicates that your wife does not exist separate from or outside of you (if you didn't exist, can you be certain that your wife would exist?). It indicates that there is no outside of you, that you are the knower, or dreamer as I often say, and that your wife—where she is, what she's thinking about, how she's doing—is appearing within you like a dream. Rather than "out there" somewhere, even the world and its 7.5 billion human beings are appearing within you.

If you swap belief for experience, what's undeniably revealed is that you are not a separate human being. You are Being itself, Consciousness. And the world appears within this Being.

Incidentally, knowing that the world appears within you like a dream facilitates love, including the love you share with your wife.

"I'm not my thoughts; I'm not my feelings"—I hear this all the time, but it never helps me. Why do I usually feel worse, or super tense, when I try to not be my thoughts and feelings?

You're trying from the illusory perspective of a separate self or body, which is impossible. As you've experienced, this effort compounds suffering because the belief or misunderstanding that "I am the body" is the origin of suffering.

When teachers, or anyone, state that "I am not my thoughts and feelings," what they actually sense is that while thoughts and feelings arise within us, they don't arise within a body—what we've been trained to believe ourselves to be. They arise within the whole, the true Self.

In other words, if personalized, thoughts and feelings become problematic. If not personalized, they don't.

What does it mean to "die before you can live"?

It means the breaking down of belief after belief on the way to the death of the primary belief, "I am the body." Then, knowing ourselves as infinite and eternal Consciousness, we head back into the world freely and lovingly. This is the intention of self-exploration. (And the intention of this book.)

Do we really have any way of knowing who or what is having an experience?

Logically speaking, since a separate self has never been found, it's not a separate self that experiences. Who or what else could it be? The constant to all experience is Consciousness, or, if you prefer, Awareness. An experience could not be had without it.

So Consciousness must be who we are, and all experience must be on behalf of Consciousness.

One surprising thing you've mentioned is that—similar to relationships, fame, and money—"states of mind" are also objects we seek. I was taught that my experience was a function of my state of mind. Are you proposing something different?

All objects are known. Substances are known, relationships and people are known, fame and fortune are known. States of mind, too, are known. These objects arise and fall within, and are made of, the only knower—Consciousness.

A state of mind, then, is not something owned by a person. A state of mind is a transient modulation of Consciousness. It has no function or power per se. How could a transient modulation have true function or power? Leave any concern about your state of mind alone.

Is it possible to take action, but not on behalf of a separate person or self?

Actions aren't taken on behalf of anyone or anything. They appear and disappear indiscriminately within the whole, Consciousness. Even the thought that "I am a separate self named 'John' who takes action" appears and disappears within the whole.

While I've said that Consciousness overlooks its true nature, modulates within itself, or even heads into the world, I'm not saying that these actions take place anywhere other than within a Consciousness that does not move about or change.

To me, suffering is very real. You seem to be saying that it isn't real. Am I missing something?

If you're insinuating that you're a separate self who's suffering, then yes, you're missing or overlooking the actual nature of experience. But as I would never discount suffering, let's follow this further. Experience says that suffering appears within you. Experience also says that since it can only appear within you, suffering is made of you. Instead of focusing on the suffering of a nonexistent separate self, the question I'd then ask is this: "Who or what are you?"

You are the one in which all sensations appear; you are Consciousness.

Suffering, given that, is real. But in a different way than we think. Suffering is real because it's made of Consciousness, the reality of all things.

Several years ago, my coach suggested that psychologically I work from the inside out. Meaning that no outside circumstance could make me feel a certain way or damage who I am. This was extremely helpful. I felt good for a while. Why didn't it last? Why did it seem that circumstances were affecting me again, or that I was allowing them to?

First, you temporarily experienced good feelings not because of your coach's suggested model of how you work, but rather because you temporarily stopped seeking. Only the cessation of seeking, not the apparent reason you stopped seeking, can halt suffering.

More important, while the theory that circumstances can't

damage you has merit, the theory that you, or we, work from the inside out does not. No doubt, you are the essence of resilience, and nothing has ever nor will ever harm you. No doubt, this echo of truth was sparked several years ago by your coach. But this "you" we're speaking of is not a separate object who works a certain way (inside out). This you is Consciousness.

While well-intentioned, your coach fortified the very belief that eventually ramps up confusion, suffering, and dissension: "I am a separate object who lives in a world of separate objects and circumstances that exist outside of me."

It's not your coach's fault, mind you. There was a time when I, too, offered this type of advice. Like virtually everyone, those of us called to serve have also been indoctrinated away from our true nature.

Can you explain the phrase "Awareness, or Consciousness, is only aware of itself"?

A person is not aware, an animal is not aware, a tree is not aware, a thought is not aware. All of these objects appear within the true Self, Consciousness, the whole, you—or Awareness. All objects are made of you, Awareness. It is Awareness that is aware of these objects. So, since all objects are made of Awareness, "Awareness is only aware of itself."

The idea of being born a Catholic, Muslim, Jew, or any label seems absurd. How can a soul be born with spiritual DNA?

Your question strikes at the heart of belief, although perhaps not as you intended. That is, if you believe you were born, believe you're a separate self or "soul," then the natural fallout will be the absurdity you describe. But if you stick to experience, you'll find that you've never experienced the birth, arrival, or appearance of yourself. And a self that was never born could obviously not have been born with a label. The absence of labels, and of separation, is the essence of spirituality and peace.

What, in your opinion, is the key to getting along with others, including those with whom I may not agree?

In any relationship, before you get to know anything about the "other," make sure you know that he or she shares your Being.

"Look inward" doesn't quite add up. I've heard you use this expression, but if Consciousness is singular, where is "inward"?

Wonderful question. From the purest perch, you're right, there is no "inward" (or "inside" or "within"). There is only Consciousness. I often use this term because it's necessary to counter the deeply ingrained belief that there is, in fact, a material world "outside."

I accept that "All things are one with me, made of me" is the foundation of peace. But I easily forget. I then fall for old temptations and tend to place blame. Any thoughts on this?

We can easily fall prey to stale beliefs and materialistic temptations when they arise. That's why the support and stability of community is so vital. When I've seemed to overlook the essence of who I am, rather than placating my nonexistent "humanness" or trying to comfort me, friends have guided me back home with the utmost directness and precision. Doing so is the purest expression of the true Self. And for that I'm extremely thankful.

In effect, that's what we do as a community in our meetings, on webinars, during interactions on social media, and in private discussions. (And in *True Self*.) It's OK to forget. It happens for no distinct reason. It's normal. Like all things, forgetting is shared by all.

Knowing myself as love, why do I feel so alone at times?

You're sensing the aloneness, the solitary quality, the non-dual nature of love. This isn't wrong. The belief that a sense of aloneness is wrong leads us to seek love in objects and others, where it can never be found. Right where you are is perfect. No chasing. From right where you are, well-suited objects and others will find you.

3.

True Self in the World

The three sections of this book are illustrations of three stages of self-exploration, what we might call three stages of *awakening*. As you've likely surmised, we're now at the outset of stage 3.

But before we dive into stage 3—and the world within—let's take a brief look back at the first two.

Stage 1. The dissolution of belief. The recognition of who you are not.

From a young age, you were seemingly indoctrinated. You were innocently conditioned by parents, teachers, coaches, and other elders (who were conditioned themselves) to believe yourself to be a separate or personal entity. You have your name, your body, your mind, even a so-called "soul." It's all about you, the person. You're a bona fide individual, isolated and distinct. And if that weren't enough, you're imperfect, less than whole, perhaps even a sinner with only a finite amount of time on a finite planet containing a finite amount of resources. As such, you must avoid this and that, defeat this and that, pursue this and that, obtain this and that in order to become an admirable individual. In order to become complete. In order to find the freedom—the peace, love, and happiness—that you've always coveted.

But it all seems off. You don't, at first, have a clue about separation, lack, or life span. You experience one vast canvas with no distinctions, shortages, or boundaries. But, again, you're told that certain others—the elders and experts who are focusing on some vague material world—know better. So you fall for it. And suffer. And cope. Until you sort of don't. You now half listen when, for the purpose of knowing yourself and becoming more secure, they tell you to merge with or acquire objects (substances, activities, accolades, relationships, and higher states of mind). Then, one day, you've truly had enough. Something's definitely not right and not working. You aren't a limited body and mind (an object) who can be made whole through other objects. There can't be limits. You've never not been whole. While still somewhat confusing, this liberating recognition initiates the journey. You're on your way inward. You're on the pathless path back home.

Stage 2. The knowing of Self. The sense of who or what you are.

If you're not a finite body and mind, who or what are you? You receive clues. You still experience a divvied-up world, but something is different. You take these lines of distinction less seriously. You detect a hint of yourself in everyone and everything. The face of God, infinite and eternal Consciousness, now accompanies all appearances. You sense an absence of "I," the person, while sensing the presence of freedom. What does this mean? What is your experience telling you? Where is it taking you?

The answer:

Freedom is not a quality, state, or feeling to seek. You actually are the freedom, the peace, love, and happiness, that you've always held dear. The true Self equals Consciousness. All things are appearing within you, are made of you, and are known by you too. Jesus said, "I and my Father are one." It all falls into place.

Stage 3. True Self in the world. Living it.

And here you are. The challenge, though, has just begun. Your programming, this idea of a personal you, who you are not, will reappear. And when it does, it's essential that you be patient and cut this false sense of self some slack.

Sure, the recognitions detailed in stages 1 and 2 occurred instantaneously. You're now certain that "I am not a separate self, a body and mind." You now understand that the true Self is the very same as Consciousness itself. Yet the aftereffects or implications will be slow to seep from background to foreground. You might, for example, still take things personally. You might overreact. You might be lured by old habits. There's no fault in any of this. It's all OK. Stages 1 and 2 will not bring immunity to struggles and suffering. When the bar gets raised, challenges often seem greater, the tests more formidable. Rather than obstacles, though, you'll soon welcome these tests as opportunities to rise above your programming and stand as and share who you truly are. Then, as old wants and needs continue to wither—as you pay less and less attention to the desire for objects—compassion and harmony will become even more the rule. From the perspective of the true Self, integrity is automatic, morality a cinch. Others will take notice. How could they not? As you see yourself in them, they reflect love back to you. You're now "in the world, but not of it." You're not an object within a world of objects. All objects are where they've always been. Within you. Made of you. Known by you.

You are home and here to serve. We are home. The awakening's at hand.

LOOK TO THE OBVIOUS

The "awakening," the answer to what ails the world, is so obvious that it seems not worth the while of most people. It's so matter-of-fact that it's almost always discarded for cerebral-sounding jargon. It's so unexciting that even charisma, humor, and clever writing can't jazz it up.

But since you remain intrigued, since your calling is sacred, check out these eight basic words once again:

No object has ever appeared separate from you.

Now if you're tempted to doubt these words (which is typical even at this stage), or if you still claim that there are billions of objects out there separate from you, let's reevaluate:

Does your "billions of objects" claim appear separate from you?

Does anything that you observe, hear, feel, taste, smell, utter, or imagine appear separate from you?

Does an "outside of you" or "separate from you" even exist?

Look to experience.

All objects, all situations, all of it requires you. Any notion of a separate subject (you) and object (someone or something else) is speculation, conjecture, an unproven theory, a programmed belief.

And further, if our shared Being, and its inherent lack of separation, isn't the answer to peace, love, and happiness—then there is no answer.

We're hating, mocking, discriminating against, stealing from, walling off, gossiping about, resisting, jailing, and killing our *Self.*

We're too confused to notice what's staring us right in the face.

Look to the obvious. To what's most basic. To what you did not learn. To what cannot change. To what you've always known to be true.

No you, no world.

Peace, love, and happiness are waiting.

THE PREREQUISITE

The prerequisite is simple. Yet due to centuries of programming, it seems so far away. The prerequisite is effortless. Yet because of trying so hard to find it, it seems so far away. The prerequisite is unusual; it might seem weird or far-fetched. Yet since it takes courage to break free from the pack, to not conform, it seems so far away.

What, then, is the prerequisite for the dissolution of confusion, blame, poverty, greed, discrimination, pollution, wars, and all the problems that seem to drive people apart? What's the sole prerequisite for not only happiness, but for world harmony, well-being, and peace?

It's not a new strategy, guideline, technique, science, way of thinking, program, law, method, practice, or leader. It's not an opinion or theory.

But rather, it's this:

The dissolution of the materialistic paradigm. For when the belief in materialism dissolves, the nature of reality—Consciousness—will stand revealed.

Now is the time to dismantle the unverified framework of our culture: the belief that objects are actual entities that can exist independently or separate from us, separate from who we are, separate from Consciousness. Until we do, the mistaken premise that objects can make us feel something, make us do something, or that they're worth something will continue to reign supreme. Today, we're at each other's throats, caught up in a mad dash to acquire, build, or divest ourselves of objects (such as bad feelings) in an impossible quest to become secure.

Oh, I know. Many are already speaking out and discouraging this type of cutthroat, wayward behavior. Some are trying to teach us to manage or control it. Others are suggesting that objects can't cause feelings since feelings are only linked to our thoughts. But, as we're experiencing right now, these approaches are futile.

Consumed by the cultural misunderstanding that objects are valuable, meaningful, or real—*all* approaches are futile.

Again, consider:

Can an object be located outside of the whole?

Is this even a rational question at this point? The whole, of course, doesn't have an outside. Separate or outside objects do not exist. That's why a separate object can't be valuable, meaningful, or real. The only reality is what objects are truly made of—Consciousness.

It's inevitable. The world will not survive under the pretense of the materialistic paradigm. A misunderstanding, a lie, cannot subsist. And as we continue to place our attention on the importance of objects, we appear to be getting closer and closer to this fateful inevitability.

But I did just say "appear."

You've made it this far through this book. You're in the process of smashing to pieces the stale framework, the lie, of materialism. The prerequisite is indeed clear. Your calling is indeed sacred. Soon you will stand as Consciousness, you will know who you are, and you will readily share yourself—the true Self—with the world.

ASKING THE UNIVERSE

Have you ever overlooked the "prerequisite" and asked the universe, or prayed, for something to occur for materialistic benefit?

A personal goal to be reached, a personal want to be satisfied, a personal problem to be solved?

While the stars may have seemed to align once or twice, hasn't this personal-fulfillment strategy proved pretty much hollow?

Meanwhile, have you ever asked the universe to fulfill an impersonal request?

Be honest, probably not. Until now, even your "selfless" prayers had a smidge of self-preservation or aggrandizement in them.

It's OK. I've been there too.

But the thing is, the only prayers that can be fulfilled *are* impersonal.

Go back to "The Crude Prayer of Materialism" (p. 57). An impersonal prayer is an activity of our singular Being. It means that the one praying is the same as the one who is prayed to, that the one asking is the same as the one who is asked. An impersonal prayer signifies that the universe, Consciousness, is asking itself for the sake of itself. And starved of the personal, the universe is then capable of fulfilling what we truly long for: the knowing of our shared Being (who or what we are and have always been). Now we stand as and for peace, love, and happiness. Now we serve the world.

Practically speaking, how might this play out?

Need a friend, partner, or colleague with whom to spread causeless joy? Ask.

Need funds or resources to help feed hungry children? Ask.

Need support breaking down the stale belief and framework mentioned in the previous note? Ask.

Want to become successful, rich, and famous?

No go.

If your request comes from the illusory perspective of a separate or personal self—better to save your breath.

WHEN LOVE IS TRUE

When love is true, there will be one way to know.

Like true prayers or requests, love won't be personal.

It'll have nothing to do with interests, backgrounds, possessions, or any aspect of life.

Quite the opposite. Love will displace the object-based world.

Without rhyme or reason, love will vanquish separation and disintegrate ego.

Absent of time and space, desires will fade.

What remains will be *here* and *now*, an intimate knowing of the Being we share.

A singular Being.

Present.

Infinite.

Eternal.

Indivisible.

When love is true, there will be one way to know.

You and I will no longer exist.

INTIMACY'S VITAL INGREDIENT

Let's now touch on another prerequisite, the vital ingredient required for the intimate bond with a life partner. (The same ingredient is essential to any bond, be it one between parents and children; among siblings, colleagues, and teammates; even a bond with a pet, hobby, or career.)

Unbeknownst to many, the most vital ingredient of an intimate relationship is to *not seek intimacy with another.* In fact, looking to a life partner to satisfy any need or desire is a recipe for trouble.

Interestingly, upon making this suggestion to most audiences, I'm usually met with some version of "I thought that's what a life partner is for." And I get it. But that is precisely the reason so many relationships turn rocky. Before we turn toward another, we must know ourselves.

Partners who, for example, understand that the true Self does not lack, that it isn't inadequate, will rarely look to another for comfort or fulfillment. To them, a bond is a means of expression, not a means to seek. That's why, first and foremost, it's vital to know where intimacy is found. Not outside in the experience of a relationship, but inside, in the shared journey back to Source.

Intimacy results when we stop asking another to fill a gaping hole that doesn't exist. From the perspective of the whole—the true Self, love—every experience is closer than close can be.

LOOKING FOR LOVE

Are you alone?
Feeling separate?
Looking for love?
Searching outside?

Recall that the only thing we truly seek is the intimacy of our own Being, the salvation that comes from Source.

It is the search for love outside of our own Being, an illusory "outside," that veils love in the first place.

So, when a sense of separation appears, rather than looking toward another, turn the search back inward.

Who am I?

Who are we?

Only an absence of otherness, an abidance in the singular essence of our own Being, will bring us home to the love we've been trained to seek.

To the love we truly are.

POINTERS TO AVOID

In my experience, the most important "pointers" for a teacher, consultant, counselor, or coach to steer clear of are those that confirm that a person . . .

- Is an actual separate entity.
- Is powerful, resilient, or creative.
- Truly controls thinking, feelings, or anything.
- Has levels of Consciousness or states of mind (that go up and down).
- Has wisdom within.
- Has free will.

- Is personally responsible.
- Can save the world.
- Can be passionate about, or love, an object.

Of course, people will appear to possess all of these qualities. And sometimes, as you're about to learn in the next note, a helper will use these appearances constructively.

But for helpers, an understanding of themselves—who they are not and a genuine sense of who they are—is paramount. An understanding of Self places truth front and center. Intuitively, from the true Self, from Consciousness, springs a mutual or shared journey back home to peace.

THE ART OF CONCESSION

Why do I often talk about the nonexistence of control, choice, or personal responsibility and at the same time maintain that in order to make moral or loving choices, we must stop trying to control? Over the years, some have argued, "You're contradicting yourself, Garret. You're saying I don't have control over my choices, and then you're asking me to make the choice to stop trying to control or make choices!"

Yes, I am. Totally on purpose. Here's the reason:

To help turn you inward—back toward Source, Consciousness, or the Self—I'm making an allowance or concession to the separate self, the ego, that you've been conditioned to believe yourself to be. Because you believe you have the power of choice, I'm asking you to exercise that power by choosing to turn your back on the one who thinks he or she is in control. Then, once accomplished, the appearance of ego will dissolve as it becomes clear that you never really had a choice or were in control. The ego arises and dissolves freely.

Indeed, wonderful teachers of non-duality such as Francis Lucille and Rupert Spira, not to mention keen sports coaches (as my father was and my son Ryan is), understand and rely on the subtle art of concession. They speak to "individuals" and their apparent free will even though they know that free will, or the power to choose, is conceptual (not true). Again, from the perspective of the true Self, no separate entity exists that *can* choose. But to arrive at this sense of wholeness and peace (a lack of control), we must first appeal to the belief in a separate self and the conditioning that gives rise to it.

It's also important to note that concessions are offered strictly as stepping-stones toward the easing of personal responsibility or burden. They never add burden. For example, Jesus said, "Do unto others as you would have them do unto you" (a concession to those who believed they were separate), not to condone separateness or apply personal pressure, but to ultimately reveal that there are no "others." Today, the majority of teachers and coaches are offering strategies and mantras—"It's on you to make things happen," "Find your personal why," "Believe in yourself," or "Compete with yourself"—that reinforce the illusion of ego and the burden it wears around its neck. By contrast, while I often refer to the modulations within as separate entities or individuals, it's for the sole purpose of ending the illusory search for control or personal responsibility. Which points us back to the singular essence of the true Self, or Consciousness.

For some, moreover, concessions can seem to make a non-dual or spiritual teacher's message inconsistent, particularly in written form. A teacher, though, will get a feel for his or her audience based on the inquiries received from that audience. If the audience is consumed by the belief in separation, the teacher's concessions will be plentiful. If the audience is familiar with the non-dual teaching, the concessions will be scarce. This book is a delicate combination of both.

The art of spiritual teaching is making concessions to truth while at the same time crowding out room for belief. In other words, a concession will always point away from objects and directly back to Source.

THINK YOU CAN CHOOSE? THEN CHOOSE THIS

The next time you're stuck in ego—the belief in separation, the illusion of control—and by the same token you're stuck between choices or paths, give this concession a shot:

Choose the path that best expresses what you hold dear.

Choose the path that best expresses the essence of Being.

Regardless of your finances, popularity, security, or any personal justification or motive, choose the path that best expresses peace, love, and happiness. The path that best reflects who you are.

If you're stuck between job offers, which job allows you to simply be yourself?

If you're stuck between food choices, which food synchronizes with true nature?

The answers will be clear as day.

Think you can choose? Fair enough. Make the "choice" to stand intentionally as the true Self.

What you'll soon find is no chooser at all.

All choices, all situations and outcomes, arise and dissolve freely within.

I MOVED ON

An audience member once angrily disagreed with my statement that there's no such thing as personal choice; that a "chooser" is a concept, a concession.

I asked him, "Would you agree that your choices are based on your conditioning and biology?"

He said, "Yes, makes sense."

"Did you choose your conditioning and biology?"

"No, course not."

I moved on.

SPINNING OUR WHEELS IN PROTEST

Here's another inquiry, a less lighthearted one, that I've posed to many audiences. Almost always, it's been met with surprise, frustration, even hostility at times:

"When in history has an organized resistance—a protest—paved the way for peace, love, happiness, or any semblance of understanding?"

I know it's tempting, but as you answer, please don't list law changes, temporary feelings of relief, or your own take on justice. I want to know when, in your actual experience, an organized resistance, fighting for an object (peace, love, and happiness are not that), or a clash of beliefs has led to a long-term or productive solution. Considering the scores of demonstrations over the years, have episodes of discrimination decreased? How about abuse? Terror? Disease? Famine? War?

Now if you answer those questions and find that, in your actual or direct experience, playing the part of protester has paved a path to true change, then by all means protest away. But I'm asking you to put the ego aside and take a genuine look. Is resistance productive in the long term? Can you find any proof whatsoever that protests have led to the sense of unity that, deep down, everyone longs for?

I'm not a pacifist either. I find prejudice, abuse, hunger, gaslighting, and war unacceptable. But my purpose is to nudge all of us to look past our conditioning to what we *know* to be true. Then we'll be in a solid position to foster lasting harmony.

Here, in turn, is what I know to be true:

When I head into the world recognizing myself as Consciousness, the true Self—which, by nature, is devoid of personal beliefs and prejudices—I help the world. When I head into the world as the separate self I've been conditioned to think myself to be—which, by nature, retains all sorts of personal beliefs and prejudices—I hurt the world. And this especially pertains to those instances when I respond to an observed inequality by calling it out, as this can be the stand of love. Sometimes, though, my responses (like yours) become overwhelmed by the conditioned habit of feeling outraged and accordingly trying to fix this outrage. Out of personal desperation rather than peaceful intuition, I then mistakenly declare a need to get involved. This only serves to heighten tension.

Peace begets peace. Love begets love. Fighting for your personal perspective of what's right or wrong? You know the deal. More protests. More resistance. More fighting. More separation. We reap what we sow.

We can protest in favor of our belief systems until we're blue in the face. This has never, nor will ever, bring what we long for.

Or . . .

We can fold inward. Discover what we long for, uncover who we are. Come to see that we can't right wrongs or fix feelings that are modulations of the whole, made of the whole. Come to appreciate that peace movements and marches, as opposed to protests and clashes, are not resistance; they're natural expressions of Consciousness. Come to know, beyond a shadow of a doubt, that we share a Being with all objects and others. We can then stop seeking and *stand* as this shared Being.

And what will occur when the true Self stands as itself?

We'll be both one with and free from all that appears.

We'll stop spinning our wheels in protests that can only be aimed at our Self.

We'll be in the world selflessly.

We'll challenge, debate, and compete free from outrage and animus.

The world will change.

Love, absent of personal perspective and prejudice, will shine.

THE ESSENTIAL DIFFERENCE BETWEEN RESISTANCE AND LIVING FREELY

As I'm using the word, *resistance*—acting in defiance of an object, other, or circumstance—stems from the belief that outside forces are real, that they possess the power to obstruct our freedom and must be countered with all our might. Resistance, quite frankly, is an act of aggression, of ignorance (as in, the ignoring of truth).

But, just so there's no confusion, those who don't adhere to the edicts of our culture—for example, interracial marriage was once forbidden and it still rightly occurred—are not necessarily acting in defiance (or aggression, or ignorance). Often, they understand that outside forces are not real, that these "forces" possess no true power or influence. Those who don't blindly adhere, then, are in the world freely. Living life as only they see fit.

Resistance feeds the foundation of all calamity and misfortune: "We are separate." It's an attempt to conquer a separate self or object that doesn't exist.

Living freely fosters the knowing that while separation may be experienced, it's never a fact. Nothing truly exists to adhere to, follow, or conquer. Living freely fosters resilience, courage, and, most of all, being true to yourself.

THE WHOLE IS WHOLE

At this juncture of our journey, you'd probably agree that just as resistance is derived from the belief that the separation appearing within the whole is indeed a fact, so, too, are prejudice, discrimination, and inequality derived from this belief.

As you've gathered:

- The whole is whole.
- All apparent things are one with the whole.
- The essence of all that appears within the whole is exactly the same.

With this in mind, my sincere hope is that we'll finally stop promoting separation—or duality, or diversity—in order to end prejudice, discrimination, and inequality. That we'll stop trying to use what is not real in order to find what *is* real: peace.

Think back two notes to the concept of "taking a stand." Ask yourself:

- In my own understandable quest for justice or what I think is right, am I attempting to fix personal outrage, or am I standing as the singular Being we are?
- In the trend that I'm setting for future generations, am I believing myself to be a distinct entity—a member of a race, creed, or religion—or am I standing as the singular Being we are?
- In my reaction to prejudice, am I attacking the prejudiced and in this manner exhibiting prejudice myself, or am I standing as the singular Being we are?

It's time to *not* take a personal stand. To stop furthering the belief in separation. To cancel the scourge of prejudice.

"We" equals the whole. Part of a whole doesn't exist.

The whole is whole. We are whole. Stand as and for the whole. Always.

PREJUDICE

One more word on prejudice:

It's ignorant. Plain and simple.

But, as experience proves time and time again, we cannot overcome ignorance by returning fire, by attacking or demonizing the perpetrators. Prejudice against the prejudiced is nothing but prejudice.

Instead, what if it were widely known that "I" cannot experience an "other" separate from or outside of myself? What if "we are not two" were known as fact, as truth, and not belief?

We can condemn prejudice. We can punish the prejudiced. We can claim that "I know better" or "I am better" than someone else. Still, the only thing that will lead to harmony is the mutual recognition of the Being we share.

Nothing else will do because nothing else is true.

NOTE TO MY TEAM

A posting that's appeared in quite a few locker rooms over the years:

There are four things we know . . .

1. **The universe is infinite and eternal.**
2. **All objects appear within, not separate from, the universe.**

3. **We are not separate objects.**
4. **We are the universe, infinite and eternal.**

For athletes, #4 is the most practical of knowledge. Expressing their infinite and eternal nature on the field of play—"No matter what occurs, we are whole; we do not lack"—is the essence of freedom.

ECHOES OF TRUTH

See this quote?

> *If we're dating, I want to be your second priority. I want your first priority to be you, your ambitions, your life, and your future, because my priority right now is me and mine. Finding happiness and security alone is crucial to finding it together.**

It's a bit different from the locker room quote introduced in the last note. I grabbed it off a Twitter post that received a multitude of likes.

Like the others that follow, this quote is a vibrant depiction of how easy it is for an echo of truth, or love, to get spun toward belief. And the thing is, the message here is so darn close. Its author has an accurate sense that making another person the priority, or linking one's identity to a partner or any object, is what breeds unhappiness. Making personal ambitions and life

*Steve Bartlett, Twitter, May 5, 2019, https://twitter.com/stevebartlettsc/status/1125079566157062146?lang=en.

the priority, however, is not an upgrade from making one's partner the priority. The priority is and must always be the true Self (Consciousness, our shared Being). Sadly, the primary belief, "I am a separate self, the body," has twisted the truth and personalized this message. Only the mutual recognition of the Being we share will erase all that is personal, revealing love.

See this quote?

Everyone wants to be great until it's time
*to do what greatness requires.**

In the world of performance, this type of high-and-mighty catchphrase is a constant. "Everyone wants to be great," that's not exactly what echoes in the back of our minds. Sure, we sense the presence of something greater. This intuition is universal. But so is the programmed belief that "I am the body." Case in point: this quote. It urges us to attempt the impossible, to find greatness in and for a transient and insecure image—the body. Once we try, aimless seeking that takes us away from "I am infinite and eternal Consciousness" has begun. Besides, even at the most practical level, what does greatness require? You have your beliefs about it; your friends have theirs. Belief on top of belief on top of belief. And further from truth we wander.

See this quote?

People are either thermometers or thermostats.
They will merely reflect the climate around them,

*Joshua Medcalf, *Chop Wood, Carry Water: How to Fall in Love with the Process of Becoming Great* (Lulu Publishing, 2015).

*or they will set it. Leaders develop values and principles to live by and set the tone for others.**

Does its rhetoric reveal the perspective of the primary belief ("I am a separate self") or that of Consciousness? The answer is obvious. The quote leads us down an endless road of hierarchy, labels, and duality. People are either leaders or followers. People are either great or subpar. And just as backward: Leaders are going to "set the tone" for others to live by. Goodness gracious. This smorgasbord of biases points so far away from our singular Being, I won't say more. Except that the true Self would never classify people into "leaders" and "followers." Separation is the primary illusion and belief.

See this quote?

Essential to know, easy to overlook:
Your state of mind creates your experience.
Your experience does not create your state of mind.

Yikes, it's one of my own from years ago. I, too, was close, but so far away. Back then, "I am a separate self" still seemed somewhat true to me. So I made the glaring mistake of suggesting that a separate self or person possesses varying states of mind, each of which possesses the power to create an experience. And while, to be honest, this quote is kind of embarrassing, I now understand the echo of truth I was attempting to convey: From the indiscriminate perspective of Consciousness, all experience

* Dr. Tim Elmore, "Habitudes," the website of the Texas FFA Association, December 1, 2012, https://www.texasffa.org/news/Habitudes-Images-for-Leaders.

is the same. Suffering is made of Consciousness. It need not be cured. The primary belief once had me mixing my message. I hope that's no longer the deal.

These quotes demonstrate and support the fact that until the primary belief, "I am a separate self, I am the body," is gone, misdirection will govern. They were designed by well-meaning yet ignorant seekers (those ignoring the true Self) to benefit seekers (those ignoring the same). Ultimately, they perpetuate what they're attempting to terminate: the desire for objects, and the confusion and suffering that results.

The true Self does not share the limits or destiny of the body. Take all advice that purports otherwise with a large grain of salt.

Know who you are, first. Then be in the world.

Not as a body and mind. As Consciousness itself.

A TEACHING OF SPIRIT

Are you interested, now more than ever, in a non-dual teaching? In a spiritual teaching? In being in the world as the true Self and teaching, and living, from this spiritual perspective? If so, great.

Here's how you'll know if a teaching fits that bill:

- *It will be logical.*
  While logic or reason is often discouraged in lieu of faith or feeling, a spiritual teaching will always make sound sense.

- *It will not be materialistic.*
  The teaching will not be used to succeed, fix, improve, or obtain.

- *It will stand the test of experience.*
  Beliefs, or the acceptance of what a teacher says in place of experience, are strongly discouraged.

- *It will not intensify burden or blame.*
  The absence of personal control and responsibility, the burgeoning of freedom, are implications of a spiritual teaching.

- *It will blow your mind.*
  Nothing to add on that.

A HUMAN EXPERIENCE THAT CAN'T BE FOUND

There's more to clear up when it comes to spiritual teachings, namely:

We are not "spiritual beings having a human experience," as the French philosopher Pierre Teilhard de Chardin once offered.

We are not "a singular spiritual Being having 7.5 billion human experiences," as New Age teachings now sometimes offer.

We are a singular Being.

This singular Being has never had and can never have human experiences. Singular is singular. I/You/We are this singular

Being, one Consciousness. All things, all experiences, share this Being. All things are made of this Being.

Remember: Any belief in human experiences is conditioned. And any teaching that promotes human experiences is not a spiritual teaching. A spiritual teaching is a teaching that dissolves conditioning, dissolves beliefs, dissolves personal burden. A spiritual teaching upends any notion that experience takes place on behalf of, through, or is controlled by a "human being."

THE ALTERNATIVE

What follows is an email exchange I had with Mary, a counselor and change worker who had attended one of my talks. It reveals the potential danger in pointing toward cognitive or psychological theories (toward burden, toward blame, toward a person's thinking, or toward the need for a clear mind) as a path to improved behavior.

It also reveals the alternative.

> Dear Garret,
>
> I work in a home for teenage girls. Prior to their placement there, the girls have often lived through neglect and physical, emotional, and sexual abuse. Now in a residential setting, they're looked after by child-care workers including me.
>
> Yesterday, there was a bad incident in the home. Several of the girls attacked one of us workers. Today, I was talking about it with one

of the girls. She was full of remorse, self-loathing, regret, and guilt. I suggested that perhaps she had less personal responsibility or choice than she thought. It was her thinking in the moment that caused her turmoil and unruly actions. If she had seen the situation differently, or other thinking had been available to her, she would have acted differently. I put these ideas to her as things to ponder. It was a quiet and gentle conversation. However, in the midst of it, I was overcome by despair. I thought, "If she is somehow at the mercy of her thinking in the moment (as all of us are), how then can she find better thinking that doesn't lead to her smashing up property, abusing herself or others, and putting herself at risk of being transferred to a maximum-security placement?" I used to think that if we experience a rise in our level of consciousness, we would have access to better-quality thought and then a better reality. But in your talk, you pointed to the folly of distinguishing levels of something that is in essence "one." Still, can we access a different quality of thought? Where is the hope for people whose thinking or misunderstanding takes them to such destructive places?

Thank you for considering my question.

Best,
Mary

Hi Mary,

I'll briefly explain here. Then I welcome you to reach out to me so we can explore further.

What you're speaking of reveals the pitfalls of pointing toward one's thinking as a means of helping. "If other thinking had been available" leaves folks wondering, "Why don't I have better thinking?" or "What's wrong with me?"

Fact is, you were on a wonderful track when you said that she had less personal responsibility than she had been led to believe. Because lifting burden from one's shoulders provides the freedom and ease from which everyone's behavior improves. But then you brought her thinking, the personal, back into the conversation, and in doing so, became confused yourself. So love, hope, and your ability to guide her were temporarily lost. Confusion will always occur when a counselor, change worker, mentor, or anyone in this type of role gets personal—or tries to get to the impersonal (love) through the personal (one's thinking and behavior). It cannot work.

Ironically, behavior that's moral, fruitful, and loving does not result from attending to behavior. It results from the alternative to this personal type of approach, from the knowing of who we truly are: a shared Being. And from knowing that all objects are made of our Being. When we overlook this truth, a sense of isolation or separation seems real, so "bad" behavior becomes increasingly likely. Again, this is what tends to occur when thought is specified as a cause and cure. This is why cognitive therapy is a failed approach. This is why telling others that their reality is thought-created is a failed approach. This is why telling others that when their thoughts improve they'll feel and act better is a failed approach. These thought-centered (personal) approaches require more thought, more exertion. They further veil the Being we share.

Far from an emphasis on thought, Mary, show others, in your own way, what you know deep in your heart: that they are not truly "others." This knowing represents the absence of the personal, the realization of our true essence. From there, morality and productivity become graceful effects.

Thank you for reaching out to me.

All my love,
Garret

GETTING SERIOUS

Mary took her work with teenage girls seriously enough to reflect on her own tendencies, and to reach out for assistance. She is special. Genuine helpers like Mary aren't beholden to ego or to tried-and-untrue methodologies; they're beholden to helping.

I, too, take my work—the sharing of true nature and

non-duality, encouraging my audience to know who they are and remain true to this knowing—seriously. So much so that it's not unusual for me to be faulted for my seriousness. More times than I can count, I've been sarcastically asked, "You're really into and serious about this teaching, aren't you, Garret?" You bet I am! I sometimes even wonder if I'm taking it as seriously as I should.

Now please don't get thrown by the word *serious*. This isn't life and death (there is no life and death). But what can be more important or serious than eradicating the belief that people, objects, and circumstances arise separate from or outside of you? From this belief originates 100 percent of suffering, conflict, and destruction.

Of course, the ego will rebel against "serious." The examination of Self always triggers the non-Self. The ego can't stand to be called out for what it is; such a serious examination foreshadows its demise.

More to the point, however, the knowing of our shared Being just might foreshadow a harmonious world. For if you share my Being, placing your needs above mine, or taking from you to prop up me, becomes impossible.

Taking non-duality too seriously?

There's no halfway. The direct and resolute path is serious. And fascinating. And divine.

It's the only path home.

WHEN READY

Nevertheless, it remains extremely difficult and rare for someone to take self-exploration seriously—to intentionally stand as

Source, as Consciousness, to truly know oneself—if he or she has not exhaustedly searched away from home.

So if that's you (or a family member or friend), a suggestion:

Like the prodigal son mentioned early in section 2, go ahead and search. Rummage through all the seemingly separate shiny objects of the material world.

Eventually, when all else lets you down, you'll simply turn around and be headed back from where you came.

KNOWING PEACE

- When the one who's teaching is the same as the one who is taught.
- When the one who's serving is the same as the one who is served.
- When the one who's judging is the same as the one who is judged.
- When the one who's counseling is the same as the one who is counseled.
- When the one who's parenting is the same as the one who is parented.
- When the one who's experiencing is the same as the one who is experienced.
- When the one who's loving is the same as the one who is loved.

When we know, without question, that separation, duality, or materialism is untrue—when we know that the essence of all things is the same—we will know peace.

PRACTICALITY

A former colleague, who often seemed in search of peace, once emailed me this significant question:

> Garret, all this talk in your articles and videos about who we are, the true Self, or Consciousness, is all well and good. But when are you going to get real and offer some practical advice?

"Get real." Funny. Sort of.

As you've probably grasped, it's incredibly *impractical* to offer "practical advice" (methods, tools, techniques, strategies) excluding a definitive understanding of who we truly are. After all, what good is advice if we don't know who's receiving the advice?

Check this out for yourself:

While perhaps you've made some short-term gains here and there, what permanent value has the standard brand of practical advice produced? Have you found lasting answers and peace? Or do you keep moving from fix to fix, practice to practice, mantra to mantra, or guru to guru?

I know the answer. Because if you don't recognize that the body-mind is not who you are, all this advice will do is fortify the belief that it is who you are. It will fortify the belief that you share the body-mind's limitations and insecurities. It will keep you seeking and seeking.

On the other hand, the pinnacle of practicality is discovering that who you are—Consciousness itself—is not only infinite and eternal, but perpetually whole, resilient, and free. It's this discovery, and only this discovery, that allows you to head boldly into the material world and perform, not to mention love, without restriction. It's this discovery that allows you to live "all in."

Want some real and practical advice?

Simple.

There's nothing more unreal or impractical than the belief that you are a body-mind, separate self, or human being.

There's nothing more practical than being utterly certain that who you truly are is so much more.

A TEACHER'S GREATEST GIFT

A brief practicality-based recommendation for teachers, counselors, and coaches (and also parents):

If the person with whom you're working offers an idea that is seemingly deeper than your own realm of understanding, if insecurity then arises within you, don't slough off, disparage, or one-up this idea. Don't get stuck in a hierarchical construct that, to the true Self, doesn't exist.

When I was young and I would question a more-seasoned teacher, as was my inclination, I often heard:

"You're overthinking, Garret." "Get out of the intellect." "Come back to me once your mind has quieted."

Better to try this:

"Let's explore this idea, your inkling, together."

You might have to refund some money. You might even have to become the student for a bit. But the refusal to give in to the conditioning of ego will be your greatest gift of all.

ABSENT OF THE PERSONAL, LOVE ABOUNDS

My father died while I was in the middle of writing this book. As my wife, children, and sister would attest, my father and I had a turbulent relationship at best. It was the fallout from this relationship that largely initiated my journey of self-discovery, for which he had little tolerance. Upon his passing, however, this journey took an unexpected and profound turn.

But let's first wind back the clock to when, in the waning months of my father's life, I became worried that we wouldn't clear up the misgivings between us. Even worse, I was terrified that I'd hold on to resentment toward him. (I know, I know, a teacher of non-duality holding on to resentment. Conditioning has its blind spots!) And during my trips to Florida to take him to treatment when he was sick, these fears were confirmed. He expressed no willingness for compassionate closure and no desire to make amends. He seemed unable to face it. And although I kept it to myself, my worry and resentment built and built, right up until the day my father died.

But here's the unexpected and profound turn:

With his body gone, I'm experiencing no resentment at all. Any sense of blame has vanished. Free of trying to forgive or let go, my love for my father has never been more present and powerful. It's virtually impossible to conjure up a memory with pain.

What's this all about?

The answer is sprinkled throughout *True Self*:

> *Absent of the personal, love abounds.*

The finite body-mind veils who we truly are. It veils love. It veils Consciousness. In other words, love is not found in a person. My father's body has left us, and the love that was always billowing below the surface is all that remains.

To avert any confusion, I'm not implying here that in order to know love, the death of the human body is required. Even through heartache, my father and I shared many loving moments where we lost ourselves in sports, in long drives to my games and tournaments, or in talks about our mutual interest in coaching (as I said before, he was one heck of a hockey coach). What love does require, however, is knowing that we are not the body and mind. Again, love is the mutual recognition of the Being we share. When the personal self, the body-mind, dissolves or dies, this shared Being stands revealed.

Unfortunately, my father didn't quite understand. As the ego, the residue of the belief that "I am the body and mind," is wont to do, it had him searching for good feelings—for love—in activities, in possessions, and in others. Particularly in me, his oldest child. This very seeking obscured his love. And to be fair, my resistance to his seeking obscured mine.

But no more.

My father and I were love. My father and I are love. And now, as I gaze at a photo of him on my desk with a tear in my eye, this love is effortlessly building and building with each passing day.

WHY IT MATTERS

- Why does it matter that love builds upon the absence of the personal?
- Why does it matter to explore the actual nature of experience, rather than living a life based on belief?
- Why does it matter whether there is or isn't duality?
- Why does it matter if free will exists?
- Why does it matter to know what the mind is made of, rather than how the mind functions?
- Why does it matter whether the body is an image or an entity?
- Why does it matter whether God is a shared or separate Being?
- Why does it matter whether the world appears outside of me or within me?

It's not at all cryptic.

Those who explore the actual nature of experience—those who hold still, surrender, and make the knowing of their own Being the priority—have grown tired of seeking gratification, security, positivity, connection, popularity, purpose, and success. They've grown tired of seeking in the material world. They've grown tired of the pleasure-pain cycle, the cycle of relief followed by tension, that imminently follows this seeking. They've come to realize that all desire is a desire to know what's real. They thirst for absolute truth. And they're not going to stop breaking down belief after belief until they find it.

That's why it matters.

SPIRITUAL MATERIALISM

A word of caution as you thirst for truth:

Be careful with the New Age belief that the *essence of Being* and *material things* can be "evenly traded." The belief that Spirit—Consciousness, God—can be utilized for materialistic or personal purposes. This belief or theory, known as *spiritual materialism* (first mentioned back in "Desire and Grace," p. 72), will leave you perplexed, hollow, and exhausted.

Material things are made of Spirit. It doesn't work the other way. Spirit is not a material thing.

In this book, I reveal the implications of the knowing of your own Being, our shared Being. I portray this knowing as the prerequisite for harmony, for happiness and peace. I do not, however, prescribe non-duality, a Consciousness-only model, or self-exploration as a personal cure. For anything.

TO LIVE WITHOUT SUFFERING

Imagine a world in which no one sought and applied cures for suffering. Or fear. Or insecurity. Or anger. Or anxiety. Or frustration. Or jealousy.

Give yourself a minute.

Do you see a world at war?

Or . . .

A world at peace?

Do you see a world of well-being?

Or . . .

A world of dis-ease?

You've been taught that suffering must be managed or willed away. Every expert under the sun claims to have the method that leads to a tranquil mind, to peace and well-being. But let's turn to experience once more:

Have these methods, in the long term, proved effective?

Why, then, do we keep seeking the thing that will end our suffering?

Could it be that it doesn't exist?

The smartest intellects in the universe (philosophers, clerics, inventors, doctors, neuroscientists, researchers) have done their best to solve the riddle of suffering. Tons of ideas have been proposed. If suffering could be cured or even managed with any consistency, wouldn't we have figured it out by now?

And even more critical, could it be that the suggestion that suffering must be fixed, and attempts to fix it, are contributing to the disharmony of our culture? Could it be that seeking materialistic causes and cures for suffering leads to more confusion, blame, and our widespread habit of lashing out?

What if to solve the riddle of suffering, we must consider the opposite approach? What if to live without suffering, we must first be willing to live *with* suffering? Again, nothing else is doing the trick.

The next time suffering arises, think twice about your impulse to run, hide, medicate, arm yourself, temporarily distract yourself, or hunt down the cause and the cure. See what living with suffering actually brings.

In the absence of seeking a cure, perhaps you—and the world—will find peace.

SIMPLY PAUSE

Along the lines of living with suffering, the next time the urge of an old and unwanted habit strikes, instead of reaching for a fix, here's another reminder meant to draw your attention back to peace, back to the singular essence of all things:

> *Simply pause.*

If the urge remains, pause again, and keep extending the pause until the urge no longer belongs to a person.

That's right.

Until it becomes clear that the urge is a modulation within you, made of you, known by you—Consciousness.

No urge (feeling, sensation, or any object or modulation) has been found *within* a person. So if not personalized, the urge will be welcomed by the Consciousness in which all modulations are found.

It will then dissolve back into its own essence.

THE UNLIKELY TRIO OF CLIMATE CHANGE, PIERCE BROSNAN, AND THE BELIEF IN SEPARATION

In May 2019, the actor Pierce Brosnan gave a moving commencement address at my daughter's college graduation. It turns out he's an environmental activist working hard to save the earth from "climate change." He exposed all the issues that day, including the "bad people" at fault for environmental degradation, those we must resist in order to turn the environment around.

But, with all due respect to Mr. Brosnan's efforts, here's something that I'm hoping this book has made evident:

A damaged environment is not the result of bad people. It's the result of the near-universal conditioning that has us believing we are individual people, separate selves who lack. This belief has virtually everyone taking from the environment, and some fighting to protect the environment, to fill this sense of lack. Environmental degradation is but one of the many effects of the belief in separation, the belief that the true Self shares the limits and fate of a human being.

This is why—even though I, too, want the environment protected—I'm mostly committed to pointing my audience away from the blight of this materialistic belief. No one has found a separate self, object, or world. Experience is screaming out to us that separation, materialism, doesn't exist. We are infinite and eternal, and so is the environment.

Fact is, many of those with whom I work have tasted freedom, passion, purpose, and a love for all things by exploring the infinite and eternal nature of the true Self, by recognizing the indivisible nature of what is whole. To "save" humanity and the planet, then, we must first disregard the belief that we're anything but whole. Survival of the fittest—or the need to take from/hurt others or the planet—will then be seen for what it is: an unfounded theory whose days are short.

The solution to the so-called "climate crisis," all cards on the table, is not built upon a foundation of science, politics, or good ousting bad. It's built, like all else, on understanding who or what we are. On knowing ourselves. It's simply impossible for the true Self, Consciousness, to do damage.

Pierce Brosnan rallied a group of young college graduates that day in May. Toward materialism, that is. He unknowingly backed the belief in separation, in division. He fortified the illusion of blame. He mobilized an innocently ignorant mentality of "us versus them." And we've all done the same.

We share a Being. We—and the environment—are this Being. And everyone knows it deep inside.

It is on the foundation of this truth, and this truth alone, that we'll treat the environment as we treat ourselves, so the healing can begin.

REST IN THE ORDINARY

Unlike the excitement of a battle, protest, or the mobilization around any materialistic cause, there's nothing at all extraordinary about the true Self. No bells and whistles, no intensity, no wow, no nirvana.

Quite the contrary, actually.

Who we are is so basic, so normal, so ordinary that it gets overlooked in favor of us seeking the extraordinary experiences, the thrills and chills, of the material world.

But, my friend, rest in the ordinary.

Keep in the stillness.

Know thyself.

Then travel within.

Only when the material world becomes ordinary too—when the highs and lows diminish, when all things blend in unity—will we be in a position to love and to serve.

YOU CANNOT GAIN WISDOM FROM OTHERS

While you can and should explore with others, with those who stand ready to love and to serve, here's another implication of knowing thyself:

> *You cannot gain wisdom, or obtain truth, from others.*

For that to be possible, you would have to be an "other" yourself—separate from the others you assume are providing you wisdom.

But you are not. And if you overlook that you are not, if you take yourself to be an other in a world of others, you run the risk of adding belief, of adding programming or indoctrination. You're in jeopardy of fortifying the very root of the confusion and suffering that has you seeking wisdom from others.

Want to gain something? Obtain something? Or, preferably, break down something old?

Brilliant.

Then notice, and savor, that every revelation apparently gleaned from another is followed by:

"Gosh, I've always known that to be true."

COURSES

The noted psychologist Dr. George Pransky and I once explored the value of certification courses and other programs that train teachers to teach, coaches to coach, and psychologists to be more proficient psychologists.

Talk about trying to gain wisdom from others!

The implicit claim made by those running these courses is that by introducing participants to truth-bearing and life-changing concepts, they'll be in a better position to help others. Some also claim that they can assist participants in building their practices or businesses.

I was not in favor of these courses then, and I'm not in favor of them today.

Here's why:

They don't work. While a course may be enjoyable, afford a sense of belonging, or offer a temporary distraction, if your proficiencies don't include the ability to teach, coach, or counsel, this will not change. No course or course leader can enhance what you don't possess.

What's more, those running these courses or programs should

take a hard look at themselves. Hinting at outcomes is a slippery slope that the ego relishes. If you're a teacher, coach, or counselor and believe that a certain approach or realization has worked for you (perhaps boosted your mood and life), great. But you have no proof that your belief applies to others. On top of that, the insecurity arising within you, the insecurity you're attempting to placate by sharing your belief with others, is your sign not to.

This note is a direct plea to those running these types of courses, to experts and self-help professionals: Please consider something vital. What exactly are you promising? Can you promise anything more than your unwavering love and support?

And to be clear, I'm including myself in this inquiry. Can I promise a client, organization, or audience the keys to well-being or success? Of course not.

Group leader, teacher, coach, or counselor: These are the most trusted of titles. People reach out to you because nothing has proved effective. They're afraid, desperate, gullible, and will do anything to not live this way. If you hold one of these titles and you're ensuring results or implying that you have the ability to inspire someone to a more purposeful life, you're betraying this trust. If you're showcasing your own charisma, wit, stories, relationships, or achievements, you're betraying this trust. If you're using a basic knowledge of human frailties as a concealed and perpetual marketing tool, you're betraying this trust. If you're intimating that your approach is the answer to any personal objective, you're betraying this trust.

Every person who walks through your door is seeking the road home, the road to peace, love, and happiness. They just don't know it. This road can't be found in you, your beliefs, or a certificate. It can't be found in thoughts, feelings, states of mind, camaraderie, wealth, or anything else from the object-based world.

If you and your course, or your work or life in general, are bolstering the very foundation of suffering—a yearning for and devotion to objects—I ask you to reconsider.

If you do reconsider, but the pull toward objects remains, that's OK. But let's talk.* An understanding of Self is especially pertinent for helpers.

MONEY ADVICE, IN BRIEF

Every day, new courses and advice appear, showing us how to make more money.

Let's not take the bait.

Until we discover that a lack of money stems from the conditioned belief that we're un-whole, our conditioned lack of abundance, we'll continue taking course after course and applying tip after tip. We'll continue spinning our wheels.

As with all objects, money is a figment of Consciousness.

And Consciousness is abundant. It's infinite in supply. It can never run out.

DON'T PREACH

In my experience as both a teacher and a sufferer, when people fall prey to their conditioned lack of abundance—when they're suffering—it's not the time to preach to them about what causes suffering.

---

*Please contact me through my website, garretkramer.com.

If, like you, they were in touch with an understanding of where "suffering" comes from, they wouldn't be suffering in the first place. Not to mention that this way-too-common practice sets up an "I know better than you" hierarchical relationship: "Here's why you're suffering and I'm not." It magnifies separation, the appearance that a teacher and sufferer are "two."

Rather, who are *we*?

In your own wonderful way, point inward to love, to Source, to the Being we share.

All answers, including the dissolution of suffering, are mutual.

NO MATTER THE EGO, HEAD FOR HOME

Throughout history, and in all fields, a select few have challenged the norms and ways of thinking of their era.

You know some of the names: Jesus, Galileo, King. In the face of vast backlash, these innovators and change agents fervently shared their philosophies and concepts. They helped strip bare our culturally conditioned beliefs. They lived life as they saw fit.

What you might not know is that the basis of our exploration—non-duality, the Consciousness-only model—has also been the subject of vast backlash.

We've discussed why:

In order to maintain its apparent existence, the ego will resist or kick back with vengeance. It will accuse the one who points toward Source, the change agent, of foolishness or not living in the real world. It will label the change agent as woo-woo, impractical, divisive. It might poke fun, belittle, or scorn.

Even in "spiritual communities"—groups that seek solace in spiritual doctrines or principles; groups that worship artifacts, VIPs, or various versions of God; groups that promote the power to control one's thoughts, words, and deeds—this vindictiveness takes place. These are communities that legitimize the belief in separation. When the ego thinks its days are numbered, it declares war.

And so:

If you've come to appreciate that the body-mind is not who you are, if you understand that the true Self does not share the limitations and fate of the separate self, and if you now realize that the essence of Being is singular—that "I and my Father are one"—be prepared. Backlash is coming.

This backlash, however, is not what it seems.

It's not really war. It's not really disagreement. Such things require separation, duality, you must have "two." Duality is only real to the ego.

Instead, the building backlash is a necessary aspect of the journey home. It will challenge your knowing. It will push you past barriers. It will further undo programming. The ego's backlash appears for one fortuitous and now welcomed reason—you're no longer seeking in the object-based world. Materialism has lost its luster. You're on the right track.

Seemingly forever, you've had the inkling that there's more to the body and mind, more to life, more to the appearance of separation than meets the eye. Keep exploring this inkling with all your heart. Regardless of the paper tiger called "ego," continue to explore. If support is needed, look to your friends on the direct and pathless path.

To no avail, the world has repeatedly turned outward to objects and others. It has avowed for long enough that answers are found in a human experience that doesn't exist.

Your duty, your sacred calling, is to set a resolute example. To, no matter what, courageously head for home.

SHARING TRUE NATURE

The notes in this book are an invitation. Rather than supporting the seeking of comfort, purpose, or love in the material world, you're being invited to turn inward. As just encouraged, to head for home. To consider that you're made of what you seek. To examine the consequences of relying on objects. To rigorously explore the Self.

These notes, however, are not meant to justify removing yourself from day-to-day life, or to recommend discarding the material world in any way. Likewise, knowing yourself as Consciousness, as opposed to a body made of matter, doesn't mean avoiding the upsets or insecurities that appear within. And concerning my work with teams or players, it definitely doesn't mean that there's a right way to feel upon a loss or a win.

All the same, some will say that the work of teachers like me, sharers of true nature, affirms that we're supposed to be calm and cool no matter what occurs. That people don't require support. That they shouldn't try their hardest. That heartache is not actual. That freedom, justice, and morality are no big deal.

But this is misunderstanding. And, more important, it's proof that teachers like me must up our performance. We must get clearer, more authentic, more welcoming. Because if our work is defined by pointing toward the sameness of all things, or about revealing that all objects (including thoughts, feelings, sensations, and perceptions) are made of Consciousness, of love, why would we not be welcoming?

Yes, in our videos or presentations, we'll make a beeline for true nature. We'll be steadfast and precise. We'll assert, without wiggle room, that all experiences appear within and are made of Consciousness. Belief won't be given an inch. But in life itself we must be open, nondiscriminatory, and understanding. All concepts honored. Inquiry, not animosity. No one blamed. All of it cherished.

Being "in life" not as a separate self, but as Consciousness itself, allows for just that.

YOUR SECRET AGENDA

A late-game admission:

I spent a good portion of my first forty years with a secret agenda driving my behavior. Even today, this duplicitous habit occasionally creeps back in.

What is a secret agenda?

It's something awfully hard to detect. Virtually everyone promotes a secret, or hidden, agenda unknowingly. But upon direct examination, you'll recognize it in a flash.

In short, doing good, serving others, or (akin to the earlier note about spiritual materialism) exploring God for personal benefit is what I'm alluding to.

A secret agenda is:

- Donating to a charity so you can feel better.
- Praying for world peace when you want peace for yourself.
- Preaching the gospel for money.
- Delving into the nature of Consciousness so you can have a joyful life.
- Joining a peace march or protest to release a sense of rage.
- Having a cleric speak to your ball club for the purpose of winning games.
- Promoting a policy to galvanize the support of your voters.
- Tweeting about your client's accomplishments as a means of trumpeting your own worth.
- Writing about secret agendas with the secret agenda of selling books or acquiring adulation, followers, and future business.

A secret agenda unavoidably takes root when our natural pull inward toward Source is hijacked by the ego, spinning us outward toward seeking success in the material world.

There's no blame for secret agendas. We're programmed to aggrandize the ego, the separate self we think ourselves to be, by any possible means. And, again, it's so easy to miss.

In summer 2019, for example, in talking about our son Ryan (who was working his way up the ranks as a college baseball coach), Liz, my wife, innocently commented, "All Ryan has to do is keep showing up as the love that he is. You never know how that will come back to him down the road."

See what I mean? The most caring person I know was oblivious to the agenda behind her second sentence. The first was textbook. Then the ego swept in with the intent of turning love into some self-fulfillment strategy. But love can't be used that way. The ego survives and thrives by taking us on mind-bending searches to nowhere. On the contrary, "showing up as love," that's the true Self in motion. That's Ryan expressing who he is rather than seeking to strengthen and enable the ego—who he is not—through his coaching.

This note is a stark, but essential, leg of our journey. We're now rounding third base. While you've been conditioned to believe that you're separate, that you're a human being who lacks and must seek in order to become whole, check in with experience. Check in with yourself. Behaviors with any degree of personal objective have yet to bring peace.

So, since they're no longer secret, when agendas creep in, let's call them out for just what they are: ego trips to suffering. You simply cannot find peace or happiness in the material world. And yet, as Liz deep down knew of Ryan, you can powerfully and movingly express yourself in that world.

Absent of a personal, hidden, or secret agenda—know yourself as love, take a stand as love, be you, and go.

Chips fall where they may.

FLIP YOUR PERSPECTIVE

You know that old coping strategy or habit (a meditation practice, a run out in nature, overeating, or promoting a "secret agenda") through which you've unproductively sought to become whole? Or through which you've sought peace, love, and happiness?

Rather than push it away or resist it, this concession might come in handy:

> *Use the strategy in reverse.*

Take a stand as peace, love, and happiness. Then, while not seeking, practice meditation, run out in nature, eat, or carry out whatever agenda you see fit.

From the perspective of "I am peace, love, and happiness," the perspective of the true Self, you'll be free—carefree, that is—to express yourself fully.

THE MODELS

That quick concession notwithstanding, it's now time to spell out how these two apparent perspectives (the personal self and the true Self) might show themselves in the material world. Surely in the years to come, you (or your family, team, or organization) will look to an expert—a teacher, doctor, coach, or counselor—for guidance. What perspective will underlie this guidance? To which of the two perspectives, or models as I present them here, will you then turn?

Model 1:

In this model, a cure is sought for the conditioned insecurity and desperation of a human being, psyche, or seemingly separate self. This model encourages the understanding and use of beliefs, values, principles, theories, attitudes, communication, leadership skills, research, strategies, and the like. Through them, a separate self can supposedly improve itself, feel better, realize its purpose, succeed, or become great.

This is the widespread personal-development model.

Model 2:

In this model, the very nature of a separate self is questioned. It starts with fundamental inquiries, such as "Who are you?" or "Are you truly a separate person?" or "On whose behalf does experience take place?" By turning inward the conditioned insecurity and desperation of a seemingly separate self, this model prevents the seeking of refuge in objects and others. Impartial to feelings, in this model, coping is not a consideration. The mind that seeks merely dissolves.

This is the extremely rare self-exploration, self-realization, self-inquiry, self-discovery, or self-reflection model. A Consciousness-only model. This model is at the heart of this book.

There's no mixing these models. Model 1 is a model of addition and veiling. Model 2 is a model of subtraction and unveiling. It's important to note again, however, that sometimes teachers of self-exploration (Model 2) will make concessions or offer apparent strategies to separate selves. But a concession will not promote the relentless seeking encouraged in Model 1. Concessions, such as the one presented in the last note, will pivot the seeker toward home. Once there, the seeker will then realize that he or she never left home to begin with.

What's more, while Model 1 comes in many shapes and sizes depending on the intellect and charisma of the teacher or group leader, hallmarks of this model are the promotion of further training and the marketing of more and more stuff to do. (Supplementary programs or certifications are an example of this.) Model 1 requires this upselling to stay afloat. In fact, this journey of addition and veiling will directly reflect the group leader's own confusion and circular path of seeking—more indoctrination, more exercises, more stories, more skills to acquire, more means through which to control, more to create, more aggrandizing the personal. All in a never-ending attempt to find happiness in the material world.

Conversely, to a seeker, Model 2 will initially appear mundane or perhaps a bit "out there." The same questions, in different forms, will be asked over and over again. Norms will be drilled down and challenged. The nature of experience attended to and cherished. The primary belief, "I am a separate self," denied. In Model 2, seeking in the material world is a nonstarter because the teacher, for the most part, is not a seeker. And if seeking does crop up, it's promptly flagged and faced. This model is not reflective of a personal journey. It's not about positivity, high states of mind, good feelings, or success. It's not about "come to me because I'm more knowledgeable than you." Model 2 represents a mutual and pathless journey back to Source. A journey shared by teacher and student. A journey without hierarchy. In Model 2, a student is only a student for a very short time.

What I'm suggesting through these two models comes down to a reminder that you've read before. Before you buy into your conditioned impulse to seek, before you turn to Model 1, ask yourself:

"Where is this impulse, this insecurity, truly guiding me?"

Or, as an alternative, think back to an illustration used in section 2 and ask:

"Am I Clark Kent, a person, or is Superman who I am?"

Undeniably, the personal-development model is prevalent. It's practically the only game in town. But how's the world faring under this model? How are *you* faring under it? The personal self craves distraction and entertainment. It needs to cope. It adores temporary satisfaction and relief. Yet tension keeps returning. Personal development is just not working. And if it were going to work with even a morsel of consistency, that would have happened already. Isn't it finally time to stop seeking a newfangled version of the same tried-and-untrue model?

Call off the search. Simply hold still. If who you are, the true Self, is limitless, is there really a need to cope, calm, or fix? Is there really a need to become more resilient, complete, or secure? Could the true Self be broken or lacking? Exactly how far away is passion, purpose, and peace?

The time has come to stop looking to experts who are more confused than you, to advice that conceals the truth that a seeker is made of what he or she seeks. You're indeed ready to discount any information that promotes seeking or following your feelings outward. You've exhausted all materialistic options. The mind can only fold inward. Everything you hold dear is found precisely where you are.

Will you look to a teacher, doctor, coach, or counselor for guidance? This can be found, but only for a short while, in Model 2.

Will you continue to look for answers or a methodology to live by? This can't be found in either model. And Model 2 will be crystal clear about that.

Become great? Follow another's ideas or beliefs? Personally develop?

No longer relevant.

You're already home.

THE BIGGEST MISTAKE

During a daylong meeting in 2018, a young man aspiring to make a career out of service to others asked me:

"What's the biggest regret or mistake you've made in your career?"

My response:

"The biggest mistake of my career—a career that's spanned nearly three decades—was attempting to serve or provide help to others when, as I see clearly now, I was incapable of providing help."

This is to say that for part of my career, I was trying to help seekers and sufferers, presuming to know what was right for them, believing what experts had told me was the proper thing to say, and all the while I was seeking and suffering myself. It's not easy to admit, but every move I made (especially in the early years) was a veiled or disingenuous attempt to fix me, to aggrandize me, to help me. I had no idea of who or what I truly was.

And now?

Truth be told, I'm still not really capable of helping others.

What I'm totally capable of, though, is undertaking a mutual journey of discovery with others. Hand in hand, we can hold still, fold inward, and explore where this journey takes us. As I hope this book reflects, we can resolutely support each other in the exploration back to the one thing we have in common—our shared Being, the true Self.

How about you? Do you, like this young man, yearn to help others? Are you currently a teacher, coach, parent, friend, or citizen who truly wants to serve?

It's OK—actually, it's wonderful—if you are. My experience-based proposition is only this:

Before you lend a deliberate hand, understand that service, or love, is nonexistent from the perspective of the personal. Understand that because the true Self cannot be broken or fragmented, it doesn't require fixing or propping up. Understand that trying to soothe another person, which requires not only perceiving but *believing* them to be a separate fragment, believing them to be less than whole, is the opposite of help, the opposite of love.

Keep exploring with rigor. Keep questioning what you yourself have been taught. Come to know who you are and what you are made of. For knowing yourself will be your greatest gift to others. This, and this alone, will be your legacy.

WE ARE NOT TWO

Are you, in the innocent spirit of service, promoting togetherness? Are you trying hard to understand, unite with, or even love your fellow human beings?

This effort is common. No doubt, noble.

Yet—and see if your experience lines up—with this effort comes frustration.

And confusion.

And struggle.

And bias.

And blame.

And conflict.

With this effort comes precisely the opposite of your original objective.

But why? Why is coming together the most difficult of tasks?

Consider, if you will, that it's merely a belief that we *can* come together. And this belief is founded on a more fundamental belief. You know the one—the belief in separation. The belief that we're a culture of individuals, a culture of separate human beings.

And from this belief our turmoil ensues.

All of it.

Bear with me here. I'm not going to have many more chances to ask. But look closely. Has a separate human being or self ever been experienced?

Zero times. Nothing has ever appeared separate from you.

And what is not two cannot connect. What assumes it's separate, but isn't, will drive itself crazy seeking connection or endeavoring to become whole.

So why not leave relationship, connection, deep listening, and all the togetherness mantras aside once and for all? Let's, for real, stop trying to serve others minus an understanding of ourselves.

Who am I? Who are we? Aren't all people merely images (or personifications) appearing within, not separate from or outside of, the same infinite and eternal space? Aren't all people made of this space?

Like whirlpools in the sea trying to come together, we're a mass of vibrations made of the whole, believing we exist apart from the whole, trying to unite in order to become whole.

This is the crux of our wheel-spinning and frustration. Throughout history and right up to today, this is what ails us. The belief that the appearance of separation equals separation, the misunderstanding that separation is real, the presumption that experience takes place on behalf of or through a body, is the foundation of all conflict.

A whirlpool is made of the sea. Not separate from the sea—it *is* the sea.

We are not two. Or ten. Or seven and a half billion.

It's perfectly appropriate to make use of the concept of

separation as necessary: to have a pleasant conversation with someone, to go for a walk with a loved one, or for any behavior that seems to require two or more people. But a belief in separation? Leave that behind.

Stay with experience. Stay with what's true.

Know yourself.

Know peace.

Know love.

Know happiness.

There's no need to unite.

PERSONALIZING THE IMPERSONAL

While on my way to give a talk, I noticed I was both a bit tired and short on time, so I stopped to buy an organic and supposedly healthy energy bar. (Confession: I'm kind of a health nut.) I resumed driving, took a bite of the bar, and immediately experienced the conflicting sensations of a sugar rush and the strong urge to take another bite. I say "conflicting" because the sugar rush certainly couldn't be cured by taking in more sugar. I mulled over this conflict, and then without thinking placed the bar on the passenger seat of my car. Surprisingly, both the sugar rush and the urge for another bite were soon gone. The once-bitten energy bar remained there the rest of the ride. I wasn't the least bit tempted.

You might be wondering, "What does this story have to do with the true Self?"

Plenty.

We either personalize experience or we don't. When we fall

prey to the belief that thoughts, feelings, and sensations occur inside a person or body, we suffer and seek relief. When we wake to the fact that thoughts, feelings, and sensations arise and dissolve within the true Self, within Consciousness—that we are enduringly experiencing the inside of Consciousness—we no longer seek at all.

My experience that day is telling. On behalf of a "tired person named Garret," the urge to fix required immediate action, which only led to a greater urge and craving. On behalf of the true Self, however, the urge was welcomed, not as a call to fix but as a mere modulation of the Self that was swiftly absorbed into the whole.

This explains why, practically speaking, we can't will or strategize ourselves through a situation like this one. And why habit-ending methods or techniques are ultimately ineffective. If we believe an urge arises in a body, if we mistake the true Self for a personal self, if we personalize the impersonal, then we will always seek relief. Yet when we realize that all experience is impersonal, that an urge is made of the Consciousness within which it appears, then seeking relief becomes moot because an urge is no longer something *to* relieve.

Where do thoughts, feelings, and sensations take place?

On whose behalf is an experience occurring?

Is it logical to resist an experience? To seek a better one?

As always, our highest calling is to continually explore these essential questions.

Which is, of course, what my talk that day was all about.

And it was wonderful. The day flew by. No energy bar required.

THE CYCLE OF ADDICTION

Another implication of the fundamental or primary belief in separation, the belief that experience occurs on behalf of a separate self, is addiction.

We're addicted to:

- Substances
- Money
- Drama
- Practices and rituals
- Social media
- Religion
- Popularity
- Escaping addiction

In fact, we're so addicted that we often exchange "destructive" addictions (a drinking or drug habit) for "constructive" addictions (exercise, a self-help modality, praying to God, checking in with a sponsor). I have an acquaintance, for instance, who dropped booze, only to consume kombucha tea like it's going out of style.

But why?

Why can't we just shake our habits altogether?

No shocker. Believing that "I am a separate object in a universe of billions and billions of other separate objects" is unnerving. Especially when nothing could be further from the truth. We're confused. We suffer. We seek relief.

In other words, the foundation of addiction or habit is a belief in the personal. The belief that thoughts, feelings, and sensations take place within a human being. The belief that we're in control. The belief that fate is in our hands. The belief that we're personally responsible. Addictions are merely the mechanisms through which we seek to cure this sense of isolation and burden, as well as its accompanying distress.

This is the reason addictions can't be managed or cleaned up, let alone cured. As I said, we can replace one addiction with another. But short of self-inquiry and the ensuing realization that we're not personal beings, deprived of the understanding that we're eternally whole and that all experiences arise indiscriminately within us (within Consciousness), the cycle of addiction remains intact.

ACTS OF KINDNESS

Have you noticed this subtle implication of the belief in the personal: that it's nearly impossible to be kind to those with whom we disagree? In spite of the constant societal prodding to respectfully "agree to disagree" with others, doing so remains an unreachable goal. We're kind to those people we agree with, and we pretty much scorn, ignore, or pretend to be kind to those people we don't. Perhaps, then, there's something intrinsically flawed about trying to get *disagreement* and *kindness* to peacefully coexist. After all, the foundation of disagreement (and all of our issues) is a belief in the personal. It's only when we're freed from this belief that kindness, or selflessness, can truly transpire.

This is why, as I've shared, "spread kindness" mantras remain ineffective. The fundamental misunderstanding, or belief, that underlies our actions has stayed the same. Civility among those conditioned to see themselves as adversaries or distinct selves can't be managed for long.

So what is effective?

Same as always. Since kindness, like love, isn't personal but rather the natural expression of the true Self, what's effective isn't a mantra, strategy, or any approach based on the separate self. What's effective (or useful) is self-exploration. Without the knowing of who we are—that we're a shared Being, a singular Self—we suffer and seek. We attempt to "agree to disagree." We force acts of kindness. We fail. Our gestures prove empty.

All ignorance is our ignorance. All brilliance is our brilliance. Every circumstance appears within us, is made of us, and is experienced by us too.

When you get right down to it, no separate circumstance exists to agree or disagree about, and no separate person exists to agree or disagree with.

The Being we share knows all things as itself.

FREE FROM RESPONSIBILITY, ACTING IN HARMONY

As you've gathered, another repercussion of the knowing of our shared Being is acknowledging that no one is personally responsible—for anything. (Recall that we first discussed this topic at the beginning of section 1.)

More precisely:

- There's no such thing as responsibility.

- The more we appreciate this fact, the more harmonious our experiences become.

To be fair, these are sometimes a reach. Virtually everyone is conditioned to think that self-blame, or guilt over mistakes—the natural result of adhering to the belief in separation and responsibility—is a righteous characteristic.

But hang on.

If we're actually in control of our actions, and personally responsible for them, if control is a truth and not a belief, we would *never* make a mistake. No one tries to mess up. Taking blame or responsibility for something we don't control is neither reasonable nor valuable.

But if not human beings, then who or what is at the helm of this game we call life?

No one, nothing.

All occurrences are impersonal and indiscriminate acts of creation. Of Consciousness. Of God. And this understanding alone frees us from the alluring delusion and immense burden of responsibility.

Let's briefly return to the conditioning I just mentioned, that self-blame is righteous. This conditioning has also forged the near-universal belief that a lack of responsibility, or accountability, is what causes wayward or harmful behavior.

Heavens. Once more, I submit the opposite.

To take on personal burden, we must take as real the illusory existence of a personal or separate self. And taking this illusory existence as real is what provokes confusion, suffering, and harm. To our shared Being, the true Self, no separate entities exist that can harm, be harmed, or assume responsibility to start with.

Is this at last becoming clear?

Understanding that all occurrences are *impersonal* leads not to irresponsible or unproductive behavior. It leads to the freedom from which we act in harmony with creation. In concert with Consciousness, with God. In loving service of the greater good.

SAVING THE WORLD, KNOWING YOURSELF

Regrettably, our shared Being, and the impersonal nature of experience, is not yet clear to our culture. We're still hungering to know who we are. One way we seek to satisfy this hunger, needless to say, is through activities. Among the most inconspicuous or not obvious of these activities is "saving the world." For it appears so virtuous (see: Pierce Brosnan, p. 228).

But as we try harder and harder to know ourselves through activities such as saving the world, this knowing of ourselves—not to mention world peace—is slipping further and further away.

And yet, if we were to do nothing except immediately cease these types of activities, cease trying to save the world, it would then become crystal clear that both we and the world don't require saving. We're fine. Completely fine.

"C'mon, that's crazy," you're even now tempted to say?

I guarantee you it's not. Here's why:

Whoever or whatever you are, you have never experienced a world or any object separate from or outside of yourself. Can you comprehend how that could conceivably happen? Me neither.

Logic says that the world and you are not two. It says the world that you're experiencing right now appears within and is made of you.

OK. Now back to saving the world:

If the world is made of you, then there's no distinct world to save. Or serve. There's only you.

Now back to knowing you:

Are you limited? Do you lack? Do you require saving?

No.

You, the one in which the world appears, are both infinite (boundless) and eternal (everlasting). And this means that the world's very essence, which is the same as yours, is infinite and eternal too. As I said, we, or you, are completely fine.

Jesus warned, "No one can serve two masters." An "outside world" is terminally deficient, as it's merely a belief, mistruth, or illusion that an outside world really exists.

A "world within," on the other hand, is verifiable through direct experience. It is true, never deficient. A world within is a world of love. And love treats all things, including the objects of the world, as an effortless expression of itself.

Know yourself, know the world, continue to express yourself, and love, freely. No seeking, or saving, is ever required.

GOD AND SUFFERING

Why, then, does there appear to be so much suffering in the world?

Why would Consciousness, or God, allow disharmony, conflict, and atrocities to occur?

Indeed, these questions have plagued theologists since, well, forever.

But that's only because the belief in separation, duality, or materialism—and the collateral belief in cause-and-effect—has plagued the world forever.

But for us no more.

God doesn't allow anything. God doesn't control anything. God doesn't cause anything. God isn't a separate or distant entity steering the course of evolution. People are not puppets.

How do I know?

I've explored direct experience. I've never experienced an object separate from or outside of myself. Including the God I was told to believe in and worship when I was a kid. I am this God. We are this God. The true Self is all there is.

And suffering?

It arises when, for no rhyme or reason, I overlook that the true Self is all there is; when I overlook the singular essence of experience; when I overlook that the world and its inhabitants and events are not real. They're nothing more than appearances. They're made of God, of Consciousness, of me.

Why does God allow suffering?

Suffering is not a thing that God decides to allow or not allow. Suffering, too, is made of God.

While never being dismissive of any appearance, or occurrence, that arises within, especially the suffering of others, let's muster the courage to say:

"God does not know suffering as suffering."

For God neither knows nor allows what cannot exist as separate.

THE QUESTION THAT ANSWERS ALL QUESTIONS

The question that answers all questions, the fundamental question, is one to which I've referred and asked several times throughout our journey. After all these years, reflecting on it still remains a staple of my day:

Does experience appear outside of you or within you?

If the former, you're a separate self in a world of separate objects. If the latter, you're the infinite and eternal Being within which a world of separate objects appears, out of which a world of separate objects is made, and with which a world of separate objects is known.

The mainstream would say the former.

What do you say now?

DON'T TRASH A FAITH

Jesus Christ knew he was God. So, wake up and find out who you really are. In our culture, of course, they'll say you're crazy and you're blasphemous, and they'll either put you in jail or a nuthouse. However, if you wake up in India and tell your friends and relations, "My goodness, I've just discovered that I'm God," they'll laugh and say, "Oh, congratulations, at last you found out."

—Alan Watts

In late 2018, in response to one of my social media posts, I received this text message from a friend who makes his living as a motivational preacher:

"Hey G, don't trash a faith. What you're suggesting is blasphemy."

I had not trashed a faith.

What I had done (in this particular social media post, as I did two notes ago) is make this fundamental suggestion: "I am Consciousness. I am God."

And until separation is actually experienced, until a self, world, or God is located separate from or outside of the whole (the whole, then, would no longer be whole), what I'll continue to do is call out the misunderstanding that "I am a separate self, who lives on a separate planet, who prays to a separate God."

Sure, I'll leave myself open to the miracle that someday, some way, separation might be experienced. But here and now, I'm breaking down the beliefs accumulated since I was a kid. And I've asked you to ponder the same. My recurring suggestion is to not believe anything that anyone tells you. Truth cannot be found in belief.

What's more, it's not trashing a faith or blasphemy to know that "I am the whole." What's blasphemy is the belief that "I am a separate self." To consider yourself separate is to limit the infinite aspect of God.

Check in with experience:

I am separate.

Or . . .

I am the whole.

Which is blasphemy?

We can keep living from belief. Living as separate entities. Trying and trying to connect.

Or . . .

We can recognize who we are. Recognize that we're a single, indivisible Being.

One is a perspective of isolation.

The other a perspective of inclusion, of love.

Trash a faith?

There's no separate faith to trash.

"I and my Father are one."

I AM THAT FRIEND

I am that friend you didn't think possible.

That friend who appears normal but many think is intriguing, eccentric, and perhaps provocative.

That friend who is no more enlightened, knowing, or special than the rest.

That friend who will not distract you from your troubles.

That friend who has no theories, substances, or materialistic techniques to sell.

That friend who perceives no enemy to defeat, no cause for which to rally, and no group, race, or nationality to exalt.

That friend who will not pander to beliefs or make allowances for "I am the body, my past, a name."

That friend who will not commiserate. No "I get how you're feeling because I've been there too."

That friend who lacks tolerance for drama, gossip, or self-serving chatter.

That friend who calls you out but will not blame.

That friend who understands when old habits flare.

That friend who both whispers and shouts, “Hold still. No more seeking out there.”

That friend who points in a contrary direction—inward, or back home to Source.

That friend who merely inquires, “What’s never been absent? Who are we?”

That friend who asks you to intentionally stand as love, to make the choice that best represents peace.

That friend who challenges you to look deeper. To explore with vigor. And then to explore with vigor some more.

That friend who resolutely supports you when our culture ridicules, shames, and condemns you for not following the herd, for being true to yourself.

That friend who is not a friend.

That friend who knows that friends don’t actually exist.

That friend who knows that “friends” are appearances, modulations, or personifications within the infinite and eternal whole. Within the singular Being we share, within the one Consciousness we are.

That friend who knows only love.

That friend who reminds you that suffering is not what it seems.

That friend who wakes you from your dream.

That friend who lifts the veil.

I am that friend.

I am the true Self.

I am God.

I, my friend, am you.

A MEETING OF MINDS

Do you, my friend, seek a meeting of minds?

What I mean is:

Do you follow the frequent advice to seek agreement, compromise, or conciliation with your spouse, partner, parents, siblings, children, or any "other"?

Not finding it?

That's because a meeting of minds can't be found in agreement. For agreement, you need duality. There must be two. And from the perspective of "two" comes self-preservation, and soon conflict.

This illustrates why we have all sorts of so-called "agreements" in place—rules, contracts, oaths, borders, treaties, handshakes; in the United States, we have the Constitution; in religion, we have various holy books—and still, harmony is fleeting at best.

How, then, can we arrive at a meeting of minds?

We stop seeking agreement. Without the knowing of our shared Being, seeking and discord will persist.

Instead, solve the mystery of who we are. Only that which shares a Being with all minds, or others, can know harmony. Long after you put down this book, keep on inquiring:

- Don't all disagreements come from a conditioned, or personal, perspective and not from the perspective of truth?
- Is anyone definitively right or wrong?
- Is our primary experience one of disagreement or, for that matter, agreement?

The dissolution of separation, a meeting of minds, and then harmony all arise from self-inquiry and the eventual knowing of the Being we share. This Being is love.

THE SEARCH IS OVER

With a dash of poignancy, this is my final "short" note. A note to remind you that there's nothing outside of you that can help you.

There is no outside.

To remind you that there's nothing inside of you that can help you.

What's inside of you is you.

To remind you that the search is over.

You *are* the peace, the love, the happiness—the resilience, the freedom, the passion—for which you have always longed.

TO OUR YOUNG

The preceding reminders pertain to our young people too. Accordingly, this note may be the most important in this entire book. Heck, it may be my most important writing ever.

So to those who are young, from the bottom of my heart, here goes:

- Keep speaking up.
- Keep expressing yourselves.
- Keep being you—only you.

Now I'm not, of course, talking about resistance. Trying to resist or reject is never in your best interest. What I'm talking about is not following others and their materialistic crusades. About not believing anything you see, hear, or read. About not trusting blindly. About remaining critically curious. I'm talking about being true to yourself. This is not because others are ill-intentioned. Please don't get distracted by the impossible—analyzing the mind of someone else. It's because truth can only be found in one place: your own experience.

For instance, ask yourself:

"Does what I'm being told or taught line up with what I understand to be correct? Or is it merely that person's belief?"

This goes for science as well. Just because science offers an explanation of how objects supposedly interact does not make the explanation true or reliable. This also includes me. Don't believe what I've said in this note or book. Don't believe anyone. Explore for yourself. To believe is to not know. And you do know. You, yourself, are the knower. If you'd like support, that's fine and perfectly normal. Simply stick with those who are willing to share a mutual exploration with you. An exploration free from hierarchy. Stick with those who aren't trying to sell you something, convince you of something, or program you to do something. Stick with those who, like you, are less about *seeking* who they are in the world and more about *expressing* who they are in the world. For this is the only way to set a purposeful, authentic, and tireless example. This is the only way to serve.

As I said, no matter the situation, keep being *you*. The true Self always has your back. It will never, ever let you down.

WE WILL SURVIVE

In the second note of this section, I reasoned that the world could not sustain itself under the rule of materialism. In this note, I'll provide some further clarity and perspective. (It's telling that I write these words on January 24, 2021, smack in the middle of what many are calling a "global pandemic.")

To the point: Absent of the recognition of the Being we share, not only will a marriage, family, team, community, or country ultimately collapse under its own weight, but the same will happen to humanity. Materialism, as I've insisted, is a paradigm of disunion, a model of conflict.

And yet, please don't fear.

While the belief in separation—that objects have an independent existence and value, that "*here* is me and *there* is everything else that is not me"—will indeed run its course, Consciousness will remain perfectly whole, completely undisturbed. In other words, while the materialistic model will come to an end, and perhaps so will life as we know it, our infinite and eternal Being will remain precisely as is. We will survive.

As you might imagine, this contention is often met with indignation. "Garret, do you even care about life on Earth?" is a common critique.

I'll respond to that later. First, more clarity and perspective:

There are two potential outcomes for the world. It will implode along with materialism, or, if the belief in materialism is eradicated, it will go on without it. But either way, as I just brought up, nothing can diminish, harm, or alter the infinite and eternal space in which the world appears. Nothing can wipe out Consciousness. The true Self is indestructible.

This being the case, a few questions:

Why do so many of us regularly act from fear or apprehension? Why does the world at large keep doing its darndest to rid itself of suffering? Why do we desperately seek to become whole when nothing that occurs in experience can make us un-whole? Isn't it nonsensical to fight a demise that can't actually occur? Virtually everyone today is struggling to protect themselves, to find security, to find salvation—and for what purpose?

To exemplify this pervasive lack of understanding of who we are and what we're made of (from which our tendency to act from fear originates), let's return to the mad-dash mission that many are on to save themselves by saving the world. As I said, they've undertaken this mission devoid of knowing that the world and all of its contents are made of the infinite and eternal space within which they appear. The world doesn't need to be saved. Its very essence is infinite and eternal. Our very essence is infinite and eternal. It's solely the belief that the Self is finite and limited that has human beings polluting, draining, and abusing the resources of the world in the first place.

And how about this constant political debate, the one focused on which system of society is fairer, capitalism or socialism? It's neither. The unfounded belief in *materialism* breeds all other "isms," and all suffering. Because of materialism, personal safety and gratification—at the expense of freedom, generosity, and living without discrimination—remain the priority.

Imagine, then, a world in which a Consciousness-only model prevailed. Imagine if the majority of us understood that who we are and what all things are made of is infinite and eternal Consciousness itself. Would we damage the environment for our own gain? Would any person be treated better or worse than another? Would war be possible? Would we keep striving in vain to save the whirlpools within the sea? Highly unlikely.

Now look in the opposite direction. Turn back to the materialistic model that presently consumes us. Although a separate self or object has never been found, the overwhelming consensus is that separation is not just an appearance. That it's real! That all things are bona fide independent entities. And even worse, that each separate self—in each case, a self that's *never* been found—bears the burden of fending for its own personal survival. How are we faring under this model of confusion, conflict, and survival of the most cunning? You tell me.

This confusion between appearance and reality is why, rather than continuing to seek relief in objects or delving further and further into materialism, you've been invited in this book to explore the underlying beliefs that inform the less-than-desirable manner in which we're treating each other today (animals and the environment too). As you know, we've tried hundreds of behavior-modification techniques and motivational strategies. We've tried rules, laws, and disciplines. We've tried substances. We've tried activism and protests. We've tried religion. We've tried perpetual scientific investigation into how objects interact and work. We don't need to try harder. We need to hold still and get straight what objects are made of, including human beings. The current model, materialism, is failing us. It cannot stand. We are imploding.

To repeat, though, do not worry. Or, if worry (or fear) is arising, let it arise. The true Self *will* stand. And instead of acting from the misapprehension and insecurity that incited the aforementioned indignation and backlash ("Garret, do you even care about life on Earth?"), this is the truth that experience is crying out for us to remember.

Only by knowing ourselves—by realizing that we will survive and the inherent freedom that this realization brings to light—will we generate a more prosperous, harmonious, and loving world. Recognizing our infinite and eternal nature, our Divinity, is our greatest gift to humanity.

You see, I do care, very much so, about life on Earth. But it's finally time to become much more interested in what life is. It's time to set full attention on who we are. It's time to look within—the only place we can look.

For a world within is a world of love.

SO LONG FOR NOW

My parting request, as you put down this book and head into the world, is that you stop trying to serve dual masters. You cannot seek relief in or try to save an outer world and simultaneously fold inward.

All your dreams will come true. You will know causeless joy. But not until you cease seeking comfort and your identity in objects (substances, activities, accolades, relationships, states of mind, possessions, resistance, nationalism, and religion). Not until you become less interested in how the mind works, how life works, how human nature works, or how things made of "matter" work. Not until you stop trying to cure fear and calm outrage.

And not until the world within takes to heart your resolute example.

It's not there yet.

We're not there yet.

In schools today, for example, there are classes on virtually every subject. Yet rare are those subjects that point away from the theory of materialism. Rare are those that expound on the true Self. On non-duality. On Consciousness. On the essence of Being. Perhaps someday, we'll look back on this material age and wonder: "What in God's name was the matter with us? How did we fall for 'I am a separate body and mind,' an unsubstantiated belief? How did we miss that objects can only arise and dissolve within us, the whole, that separation is just an illusion? How did we take the appearance of distinct cultures, societies, races, borders, and nations to be real?"

The belief that because I am not you (not a woman, not gay, not black, not a Christian, not the same nationality) I cannot know your feelings or relate to your experience is the root of evil. We cannot use the illusion of separation to cure the suffering and conflict wrought by our devotion to this illusion. Ridding ourselves of thoughts, feelings, disorders, negative people, and even circumstances deemed to be unjust is impossible. How are we supposed to rid ourselves of ourselves? How are we going to fix an illusion?

Sadly, as long as materialism is accepted as true, this is precisely what we'll continue seeking to do. Not until we wake up to the fact that we share a Being, that the world and all objects are mere images, modulations, or vibrations within our Being, will we cease perpetuating the primary belief in separation and emerge from the confusion.

This is why, as first outlined in the Introduction, the aim of this book has been for you to discover who you truly are through the following stages of self-exploration:

1. I am not a separate self—I do not experience from the perspective of a separate self.

2. I, the true Self, am infinite and eternal.

3. I, the true Self, am in the world, but never of it.

My hope then, all considered, is that I've done my part to help guide you back home, to the nature of Self, to the essence of all things. And that moving forward you continue to boldly explore this essence until all beliefs, all transient objects of temptation, have vanished and the truth stands revealed. Rather than evolving, achieving, or attaining, your purpose is to keep dismantling. To pull back the veil. To fold into Source.

No doubt, as I've cautioned, the ego will strongly kick back. Fear will arise.

But you are ready.

The world within you is ready.

There's nothing left to resist or seek. You've emerged from the confusion. You were never a broken and needy separate self to begin with. The true Self, Consciousness, was simply yearning to know itself as itself. Your greatest gift—"I am infinite and eternal," "I am peace, love, and happiness"—can at last be rendered.

The calling is sacred. The time to stand knowingly as who you truly are is now.

With all my love and support, thank you for reading *True Self.*

Garret

INQUIRIES AND ANSWERS

Is there anything I can do—specific books to read, videos to watch, seminars to attend, or experts to follow—in order to gain a deeper understanding of non-duality or of who I am?

Write more, read less. Express more, take in less. Be true to yourself more, follow others less. You cannot become who you already are. If you simply cease trying to gain or acquire, you'll allow for the natural dissolution of misunderstandings (beliefs). What remains, then—that which can't be dissolved—will be what you were seeking through books, videos, seminars, experts, and the like.

You seemed to be one of the first in the performance arena to question the reliance on mental strategies and techniques. I now see that maybe this wasn't your point. Can you explain?

Strategies and techniques that point us toward Source are necessary concessions to truth. Strategies and techniques for personal accomplishment, gratification, or promotion should be rethought and usually not used. The seeking of such personal and materialistic objectives is the trigger of suffering.

What advice has been most helpful to you?

The advice to take advice and turn it inward. For instance, "Do what makes you happy." Instead of seeking happiness in the material world, let's turn this advice around. What is happiness? Where is it found? When you recognize that happiness is your essential nature, "Do what makes you happy" becomes a call back to who you truly are, to happiness itself.

All advice is like that. "Be secure." "Be resilient." "Be passionate." "Be free." Turn them around and you will have found yourself.

Seems to me that rarely do counselors, psychologists, coaches, or self-development experts take an interest in true nature or non-duality. Am I accurate?

Yes. It's simply not possible to endorse or seek self-development and, at the same time, explore the non-dual nature of reality. Over the years, I've had several self-development coaches attend my programs or workshops. Almost always, these coaches ended up retreating further into the self-development or self-help space.

An exploration of non-duality is about obliterating the belief in all that is personal. About obliterating the belief that "I am a separate self." It's not about aggrandizing this belief through the seeking of good feelings, greatness, or growth. If that's the intent, ego and seeking will rule.

As I get closer to a big game, my fluctuation between worry and calm is so strong. What should I do?

Let it all come. Let it all stay for as long as it wants. Who you are cannot be touched by any of it. Who you are is *that* free. Go play—or better yet, live—as your own authentic expression of this freedom.

Would you go over the difference between the strategy to "make things happen" and your suggestion to "take a stand as Consciousness"? To me, they both seem like calls to action.

Whoever or whatever you are, you have no actual power to make things happen. This directive takes you out into the illusory material world, seeking further from yourself, further into uncertainty. If you had the power to make things happen, then you would make happen whatever you wanted to make happen.

By contrast, the concession to take a stand as Consciousness is an offering to relax all efforts, hold still, and recognize that you were never lacking, you were never a separate person or seeker to begin with. You were always Consciousness.

The difference, then, is found in the intention. The intention behind "making things happen" is needy and materialistic. The intention behind "taking a stand as Consciousness" is the knowing of your own eternal Being.

I'm struggling with whether my recent tendency to criticize government policies is good or bad. I'm getting varying opinions from friends. How do I find the answer?

Is your behavior consistent with the truth that all things share your Being? This is the most direct way to determine if your behavior has merit.

Ernest Hemingway, the famous author, declared that self-improvement is noble. Why do you share a different message?

Notice that Hemingway said "noble," not productive, wise, or even possible. Self-improvement, no matter how you look at it, is an endless pursuit. The separate self is an illusion; an illusion can't be improved. The true Self is infinite and eternal; what's infinite and eternal can't be improved either.

My son has always hesitated a little; he's afraid of getting hurt in a game. He's never had an injury, but as time goes on, he seems to be hesitating more. What can I do for him?

Appearances are deceiving. What you've described is not exactly what's occurring. His fear, all fear, stems from the conditioned belief in limitation and lack. The belief that we share the fate of the body. The belief in a death that's not been experienced.

A parent's role isn't to ingrain this sense of limitation and lack. So don't say anything about his fear of injury. As best you can, leave that be. If you address it, it will build.

Know yourself as the infinite and eternal Being you truly are. Then live this truth. Your son will be a quick study.

Your journey from mental-performance coaching to non-duality is refreshing. How do these modalities compare?

Thanks for that. Non-duality, though, isn't a modality in the way you seem to be defining it. It's a word used to describe the reality of all things, that separation is illusory, that the appearance of separate selves doesn't signify the actual existence of separate selves.

I'm also not totally sure what you mean by mental-performance coaching. I've worked with performers for most of my career, and it has many connotations. But since you described it as a modality (an approach or method), I'll go with that. The objective of mental-performance coaching is to help separate selves in numerous ways. This modality is about self-improvement, whereas non-duality reveals that there are no separate selves to improve.

As for my journey, it's the same as yours or that of anyone who's interested in non-duality. We shared the seeking of self-improvement. We now share waking up to its folly. Let's keep sharing.

After our great season last year, I'm now afraid that my players will come to training camp fat and happy. Any ideas about dialing them back in?

Just this, Coach: You're falling for the common belief that players (or people) get complacent after "success." Not mentioning this belief and your own fear of it is the best policy. Simply don't get complacent yourself. Simply get back at it with passion yourself. The players will get the message.

What, in your opinion, will happen when you die?

This is the perfect question to indicate the importance of examining direct experience as opposed to conditioned belief. That is, I have no experience of dying, so I cannot truly answer your question.

I do, however, have experience of loved ones dying. My father, for example. And while I can no longer sense his body via touch, I can imagine him, see him, hear him. No different from when he was alive, my father comes and goes frequently within my experience.

Back to me dying. The only thing I know for sure is that I've never experienced the absence of Consciousness. I've never appeared or disappeared. Experience, then, tells me that I am Consciousness, ever-present and eternal. It was the belief that I am a body, or that I view the world from the perspective of a body, that died years ago.

If cause-and-effect isn't real, then why does the belief in a separate self, and the belief in duality, seem to cause so much suffering?

It seems that way because, to a certain extent, you still see cause-and-effect as real, or as a truth. But let's once more look to experience.

Experience, perhaps unexpectedly, demonstrates that "I am a separate self" arises concurrently with suffering, not one before the other. Or you might say that a belief in oneself as a separate self *equals* suffering. One does not cause the other. And even though I often speak of causality, especially early in the teaching, the same dynamic is true of all "causes and effects." No cause-and-effect relationship is true because duality, or the existence of a separate subject and object, is not true.

Fill in the blank. The best part about your job is . . . ?

There's no best part. There's only one part, and it keeps getting better and better. My job is to undertake a mutual exploration of Self, our shared Being, with whoever shows interest.

As I continue to explore the true Self, I've lost interest in some activities and also in some friends that I've had for years. Is this normal?

Very much so. As the belief that "I am limited and lacking"—the driver of ego—loses its leverage, ego-based interests will lose their appeal. This is not to say that if an old friend needed your help that you wouldn't or shouldn't be there for that friend. From the perspective of the one who's eternally open and welcoming, the true Self, you'll act in the most loving of ways.

Your critics are plenty. Your message often falls on deaf ears. For example, environmental activists and scientists are celebrated on magazine covers, but you argue that they amplify the issues they seek to remedy. Motivational speakers tout the importance of coming together as one, but you argue that trying to come together furthers division. How do you not react to those who insult you and your writings? How do you not succumb to the desire to be more popular?

For a good part of my life, I did react to others. I did succumb to the need to be more popular. This is why my first two books presented a somewhat mixed message. Then, one day, everything changed. I can't be certain, but it seems that both my desire to appease the critics and my desire for fame faded as the belief that "I am a person named Garret" faded. And while this change has led to a more genuine message, since it's led to me being true to myself, it's also led to my work becoming less widely accepted and popular. I'll proudly and thankfully note, however, that the perfect audience is now finding me.

When you forget who you truly are, Garret, what do you do?

Garret never forgets or remembers. Forgetting and remembering, or veiling and unveiling, is a modulation of Consciousness. The best we can do is not force the veil away.

My suggestion is to continue exploring the essence of Being. The forgetting (and remembering) will soon become irrelevant. The forgetting, after all, is itself made of Consciousness.

As a concession, is it ever prudent to indulge the belief that we're each a separate self? Like in a counseling session or when with a friend.

A concession, from a non-dual perspective, does not indulge belief. A concession is simply a proposed "doing" that serves to turn those who believe they're separate back around to the fact that they're not.

The answer to your question, as you may now surmise, is no. There's never a good reason to discard the very essence of experience, or to ignore our true nature. Doing so is basically blasphemy, the ego making excuses for why its "existence" is necessary.

Your greatest gift to the world is to know yourself. All selfless, genuine, and loving acts (in counseling sessions, with friends, and elsewhere) will spring fluidly from this knowing.

Many spiritual sages claim, "I know nothing." I've never understood this claim. What's the reason for it?

There are two possible reasons. First, the "sages" you speak of are signifying that one who believes himself or herself to be a separate self, or a person, has no ability to know. The intellect is the veiling of knowing, the veiling of wisdom.

Second, pull the word *nothing* apart. "I know *no thing*" establishes that from the perspective of the one who knows, Consciousness (the "I" in this example), all apparently separate things are made of itself. There are no material things *to* know. There is only Consciousness.

So I am Consciousness, the universe itself. Thanks for that. But do you have any practical advice?

What could be more practical, or freeing, than knowing that who you truly are does not share the limitations and fate of the body, and being in the world from this perspective? What could be more impractical than thinking that you're a limited and lacking speck in the universe, not the universe itself, and being destined to a life of fear?

My players are mentally and physically exhausted. Would it be a crazy idea to give them the day off? Maybe just watch game film?

Here's another idea: Get your guys away from the facility altogether. Head to a different location. Talk about love and how much you appreciate your team, how this season has brought you closer to the knowing of your own Being. Then have each player share his own sentiments. Be sure to keep the conversation away from worldly goals. Just reflect on the only true purpose: the mutual journey to Source. The greatest journey of all.

Are you seriously suggesting that we not try to solve the world's problems?

"Problems" appear and disappear. They seem to exist and bother us sometimes, then they're gone. But what's real cannot exist only sometimes.

I'm suggesting that before we try to solve a particular problem, we should evaluate its realness or validity. Plowing our efforts into a problem that's not real is an exercise in confusion and futility.

I recently asked a psychologist about non-duality. His response: "I experience separate objects, so we're not going there. I only share what I personally experience." Do you not experience separation, Garret?

The response you received was actually ignorance masked as humility and wisdom. Of course, as the psychologist said, we experience the appearance of separate objects. But this does not make separation, or duality, true. For duality to be true, objects would have to appear separate from or outside of Consciousness (the whole). And this has never occurred.

Next time you hear, "I can only talk about what I know or experience," challenge the speaker on the nature of experience. Don't let him or her off the hook. All that's experienced is Consciousness. The objects of experience appear within and are made of Consciousness. Anyone who avoids this examination is suffering. This applies to psychologists too. Be present. Express love. You're there to extend a hand, so go for it.

Why do we need pain to know pleasure, unhappiness to know happiness, stress to know calmness, absence to know presence, bad to know good, war to know peace, and so on?

We don't.

How can I best decide whether to consider someone's advice?

Be guided by your answers to these questions: Is the advice being offered absent of a personal agenda? Is the "advice" an attempt to sell you something, influence your viewpoint, rally you to a cause, obtain you as a follower, or otherwise manipulate you?

Spiritual communities are occasionally labeled as cults. Would you explain the difference between the two?

The hallmarks of a spiritual community are logic and reason. Things will make sense. Inquiry, vetting, and meticulous investigation will be encouraged. Plus, a spiritual community is one that does not give credence to hierarchy. There may be teachers, but only for a short time. A spiritual community is one of mutual exploration and support.

The hallmarks of a cult, on the other hand, are feelings, blind faith, and belief. Ask members of a cult to explain their teaching and you'll get neither a sound nor consistent reply. Questioning is kept to a minimum. Overthinking is a common accusation. Compliance is coerced. Cults are also steeped in hierarchy, with "wise people" or an "infallible individual" at the top to be revered. This division is necessary to keep the cult, and the profiting and ego of those running it, alive.

One word of performance advice that I've never understood—and, to be honest, I've never gotten a satisfactory explanation when I've asked about it—is to stay in "the present moment" or "the Now." Why is this advice so vague?

The reason it's vague, and also confusing, to tell someone to be present, stay in the moment, or live in the Now is that this advice is almost always dispensed for the purpose of a performance outcome. Outcomes require time. The Now transcends time.

A person cannot be present. Ever. Know yourself as Presence, rather than as a person seeking to be present, and let outcomes speak for themselves.

Recognizing my true nature is awesome. But how come I still eat unhealthy food and drink too much?

Keep exploring your true nature until fulfilled. In the meantime, when you're tempted to consume unhealthy substances, gently pause or delay for as long as you can. This allows the urge to be welcomed by and absorbed back into the whole.

Rest assured, knowing yourself as love will lead to you treating all things, including the body and mind, with love.

I'm tired and I've got a game in three hours. What should I do?

You are not tired. You are you. "Tired" is a feeling that appears and disappears within you. There's nothing to do but be yourself.

Nothing I've ever tried to help ease my suffering has any staying power. Any recommendations?

Suffering cannot be concealed for long. Positive thoughts, managed feelings, and look-on-the-bright-side distractions will soon lead to further confusion and seeking, and then to more suffering.

Rather than trying to cure suffering, directly inquire about its nature. Where does suffering occur? Of what is suffering made? When you notice that suffering occurs not within a body but within the entirety of Consciousness—and so it's made of Consciousness—suffering will be greeted unconditionally and lose its grip.

Why do so many coaches and counselors have a difficult time making a living?

An industry in which coaches and counselors believe that they're "separate selves," and seek to help other "separate selves" improve aspects of their lives, cannot endure. The belief in separation is the basis of all difficulties.

It seems like you're trying to have it both ways. If you genuinely understand that there's no separation, then why are you now speaking to an audience of separate people?

I'm speaking to an audience of apparently separate people, sometimes about distinct world events, but that does not imply a lack of understanding. Once it becomes clear that audiences, and all things, appear within the whole and are made of the whole, the belief in separation (that it's real) will dissolve. But the illusion of separation does not. It appropriately remains.

I'm addressing you as a separate person, all the while understanding that you are purely a modulation (or a personification) within the whole we call Consciousness, or love.

Can human beings live in peace?

Yes. But not under the belief that you, the one who experiences all things, are a separate being. What's separate, by definition, cannot come together or live in peace.

For peace, the discovery that you are Being itself is essential. For peace, the knowing that all "humans" and objects appear within you and are made of you is essential. For peace, the knowing that all things are already living in peace must be unveiled.

The amount of injustice, hatred, and tragedy in the world is so upsetting. How can I help?

One thing not to do is try to fix your upset through a response to injustice, hatred, or tragedy. Examples of this are nonpeaceful protest and lashing out at those you deem responsible.

Feelings have no need to be fixed. They arise within you, Consciousness. They are known—not felt—by you. If you react in a quest to feel better, you'll be reacting in error. You'll then add to the tension, not lessen it.

What you can do, however, is knowingly take a stand as the Being you share with all things. You can then head into the world as this Being. From there, you'll shine as a beacon.

What would you tell a divided world?

That our primary experience or initial "relationship" with every person, animal, and object is love. Before we know anything, we know that we're an *undivided* whole, a singular Self.

Let this knowing, and only this knowing, inform and be the impetus for all of our relationships and behaviors.

REFLECTIONS

- Who am I? Baffling question, so start here: Does what you're experiencing right now appear outside of you or within you? If outside, you're a separate self experiencing a world of separate objects. If within, you're the universe experiencing a world of seemingly separate objects all made of yourself.
- If it's not obvious that the current framework for how we believe the world is built—that "all things exist separate from us"—is flawed, then what is obvious? Separation is a lie. How can anything exist without or separate from us? A lie, let alone a world built on one, cannot endure.
- Although you might find temporary relief, any distraction from suffering or coping mechanism for suffering, in due course, will perpetuate suffering.
- Truth is never learned.
- Fear arises within you. But you are never afraid. You are always you.

- Only the ego seeks positive thoughts, feelings, and experiences. Only the ego resists negative thoughts, feelings, and experiences. The true Self doesn't discriminate. It is open, welcoming, and lovingly impartial to whatever appears within.

- Preachers, teachers, doctors, and politicians who realize that human beings are naturally insecure, while the true Self is naturally secure, will take one of two paths: They'll either ask their audience to follow them down a fraudulent road to security, or they'll remind their audience of what they just realized.

- A "slump" occurs the second we link our well-being or worth to results. This means that every human being is in a slump right now.

- You cannot be both in control and in love.

- "Mindset" is a concept created by the self-help world. Believing that there's a "preferred" mindset keeps us reliant on the experts of that world.

- It's sad to see so many young adults today being conditioned to find their purpose, safety, and comfort in the relationships, activities, and possessions of the material world. Ceasing to link identity to the material world is one's only true purpose.

- Life's greatest challenge is remaining true to yourself, no matter what. Are you ready?

- Beware of the suggestion to use the knowing of your own Being for any type of personal gain. This is ignorance posing as wisdom, narcissist posing as prophet, seeker posing as sage, desperation posing as prayer, belief posing as truth. This is how the illusion and confusion of ego perpetuates itself.

- The voice in the back of your mind isn't distracting you from health, well-being, integrity, or peace. It's your everyday voice that does that.

- One thing that can be said about the most productive, consistent, and loving people is that they do not possess an intense belief in themselves.

- Among the illogical aspects of our society is that we're heavily indoctrinated to protect ourselves from death—something we have no idea is problematic—and, in the process, we deny ourselves the opportunity to live and love tension-free.

- What would you share with the world if your own fears and insecurities weren't an issue? Share that. Simply that.

- In sports, one common coaching mistake is giving players too much rest. The belief that "I am a body," the ego, is what depletes energy—not time on the court, ice, or field. In fact, players often lose a sense of ego and conserve energy during play.

- Experience is always changing. The knower of experience never does.

- Nothing you learn from another is true. "I am an American." Learned. "Money has value." Learned. "I was born and will die." Learned. What haven't you learned? Find that and you'll find the truth. About everything.

- Turn away from that which ratifies your beliefs and toward that which annihilates them.

- All criticism is self-criticism.

- Our fundamental experience is love. Because love is what we are. Everything else is learned, untrue—not what we are.

- Believe that people, animals, and nature appear outside of you, and you'll mistreat people, animals, and nature. Understand that all things appear within you and are made of you, and you'll treat all things with love.

- It's instinct to seek your Self. It's conditioning that has you seeking your Self in objects (substances, activities, accolades, relationships, and states of mind).

- Are you trying to overcome an experience? What is an experience made of? Where does an experience arise? An experience arises within Consciousness and is made of it too. Overcoming is never necessary, or true.

- Helpers are needed. What's not needed are helpers who claim to have cures.

- The illusion of ego can't rid itself of the illusion of ego. And with each action taken to enhance our personal existence—each coping technique, practice, or save-the-world strategy—that's precisely what we're trying to do.
- While it's usually a faint echo, everyone has experienced the inkling that things aren't as they seem. Explore this inkling. Don't hide from it. No matter where the exploration leads, you'll be on the right track.
- Instead of going after (and trying to manage) thoughts and feelings, allow thoughts and feelings to do what they're meant to do—come to you.
- Ups and downs occur. But who you are, the true Self, doesn't ride the wave.
- Trying to convince yourself that nothing outside of you can make you upset, nervous, or angry? No luck? That's because nothing takes place outside of you.
- Lies are detectable by the absence of logic—your own logic. If something doesn't add up, even if the majority differs, then it doesn't add up. Sure, leave yourself open to the possibility of your mind changing, but don't fake it, follow, or try to fit in. Not being true to yourself is the foundation of a life of regret.
- Concepts, such as separation, are necessary. But when concepts are turned into beliefs—"separation is real"—suffering is guaranteed.

- A cluttered mind is not possible. One at a time, a thought arises, a thought hangs out, a thought is gone.

- Here's the thing about meeting people where they are: It only works if you're trying to sell something. If your aim is to get to the bottom of something, to get to the truth or shed programming, then speak truth regardless of where people are. Those who are ready will hear you.

- We're so duped by the illusion that we're not the same that we promote diversity in order to fix the fallout (prejudice, inequality) of taking as real the illusion that we're not the same.

- To live without an anxious feeling, we must be ready, willing, and able to live with an anxious feeling.

- You cannot express who you truly are while seeking victory or success. God's infinite Being does not know outcomes.

- If you're perplexed about a situation, rather than collect and rely on research or data, get quiet and reason the situation out for yourself. In fact, you're perplexed because you've relied on outside information for far too long.

- Our most important realization? That peace, love, and happiness are available under any worldly condition. Our most important behavior? To stop pursuing peace, love, and happiness in the world.

- Losing a tolerance for drama is finding a tolerance for love.

- Achieving a desire doesn't bring relief. Achieving a desire doesn't bring joy. Relief and joy arrive the moment seeking ceases. So what we truly desire is to cease seeking.

- The secret to the game of life? To take part fully, with all our heart, while knowing that we don't control a thing.

- It's not the thoughts in your head that give rise to burden and suffering. It's the belief that thoughts are found in your head.

- Before you buy into an expert's take on a subject, and then do what he or she suggests, ask yourself, "Do I know for sure that what the expert is telling me is true?" If you don't know for sure, then don't buy in or do it. Ever.

- Often used synonymously, the words *innocent* and *well-meaning* aren't synonymous. Ego is innocent. Well-meaning it's not.

- Are you trying to become something? Fair enough. Our culture programs us to do so. Just know that you cannot become what you are not, and you cannot become what you already are. What, then, are you trying to become?

- Belief is the rationale of ego.
- We don't live in fear. We don't live in security. We are both one with and free from all experiences. All experiences live in us.
- Peace, love, and happiness will appear as destinations, but they're always our Source.
- Depression stems from the primary belief that "I am a body, person, or human being." This isolationistic and daunting mistruth accounts for all of the world's suffering. If I am a body, then I share the limits and fate of a body, and I am destined to a life of fear.
- Someday, we'll exhaust all strategies of connection and wake up to the truth: We are not two.
- At the heart of the art of coaching is the subtraction of personal burden. Talent is revealed to the exact degree that burden is stripped away.
- If you enjoy meditation, one suggestion: Place your attention not on what comes and goes—thoughts—but on the space in which thoughts come and go. Not on what's transient, but on what's permanent. You might find that meditation isn't a practice; it's who you truly are.
- Why try to be positive, confident, or calm? The true Self isn't a feeling.

- You're either protecting yourself or being yourself. Although once you get to know yourself, protecting becomes ridiculous.

- The fact that so many organizations are taught that "culture is a competitive advantage" shows that we've lost sight of what competition is. There's never an advantage in separating one group, or culture, from another. There's nothing more confining, confusing, and dangerous.

- Once a thought appears, it can't be changed or overridden. It's already been formulated and welcomed. It will fade in its own due time.

- Many of us, it seems, will tiresomely defend what we've been conditioned to believe. Trouble is, what we've been conditioned to believe isn't true.

- As you become more familiar with the nature of Self, you'll naturally lose interest in relationships that once bolstered ego. But this is a far cry from rejecting "negative" things or people. That's impossible, and actually the work of ego itself.

- The worth of a teacher, like that of a good friend, depends on whether those being taught feel as if they're contributing equally to the conversation.

- Love is alone, yet never desperate.

- It's normal to believe that we're in control. So normal that some of us actually encourage others to give up their belief in control, as if they're in control of giving up their belief in control.
- Right now, you're as aware as Awareness can be. There's no "becoming more aware."
- When it comes to problem-solving, we have the order backward. We try to solve problems so we can get on with life when we should get on with life and then see if the problems need solving.
- As you challenge and dismantle the ideas and inspirations of others (experts, gurus, pundits) that you had unknowingly accepted as true, ideas and inspirations become more plentiful, not less.
- Leaders remind others, "Do not believe me, do not follow me, we'll travel together."
- Can a thought or feeling arise anywhere else but within you? No. Has a thought or feeling ever been found within a body? No. So then who are you? Leave thoughts and feelings alone. Even the ones you've been taught are no good. Discover who you are and all thoughts and feelings will become your friend.
- Think of the opposite of greatness and be that. In fact, be so "un-great" that any sense of individuality, separation, or ego dissolves.

- Not generally seen as such, self-exploration is infinitely practical. What's more practical than knowing that who you truly are does not share the limits and fate of the body?

- First comes the coping technique, then comes the psychological issue, not the other way around. Take positive thinking. It wasn't a thing until someone decided it was better to think a certain way. Now we're on guard for our thinking, we try to control it, and we blame ourselves when we can't—which is always.

- Are you praying to a separate God for a personal want or need? It won't come true. Only when the one praying is the same as the one prayed to will peace, love, and happiness emerge.

- Prejudice = misunderstanding. This includes "thought prejudice," the misunderstanding that certain thoughts are superior to others.

- We're not individuals desiring to become more conscious; we are Consciousness. Our desire is to become less individual. We're not separate selves desiring to know God's infinite Being; we are God's infinite Being. Our desire is to know our Self.

- Many industries—self-help, medicine, advertising—are built on the belief that you're a person who lacks. No. The universe is infinite and eternal. You do not lack.

- Discrimination in the name of personal comfort or safety is the epitome of immorality.
- Although well-intended, unification mantras and strategies don't prevent conflict, they fortify it. We cannot use the belief that we're separate beings to solve the calamities formed by the belief that we're separate beings.
- Never force positivity or any disposition. Rather, be genuine, in harmony with what experience brings. Just as you are is perfect.
- I'm often criticized for my claim that "we are infinite and eternal." But, frankly, I'd rather be wrong about it than sorry for following the fear-of-death-based edicts of others, sorry that I didn't live and love freely on my own terms when I had the chance.
- Truth requires no data, no marketing, no alibi, no defense. Beliefs, lies? They take an army.
- Fearing any person, circumstance, or object (which can only be a modulation of yourself, within yourself) is the innocent working of ignorance. You are ignoring your own essence, and the essence of all things. You are ignoring God.
- At some point, virtually every person links his or her identity to outcomes. In all cases, this initiates a lifelong obstruction of potential.

- The extent of your unhappiness in the world will be directly proportional to the extent that you search for happiness in the world. The more you search for happiness in the world, the more unhappy you'll be. The less you search for happiness in the world, the less unhappy you'll be.
- What would you worry about if you weren't conditioned to worry?
- Have the courage to explore your true nature, to stay on course. Self-exploration will only obliterate who you are not. Who you are cannot be harmed.
- Yes, the mind is incapable of knowing from where it came. But not because from where it came is unknowable. Because the mind is incapable of knowing.
- You are whole. We are whole. Nothing can change what is true.
- It's common to wonder about your destiny. But it can be confusing, even worrisome. Here's a freeing alternative: Wonder about the destiny of the belief that you're a person with a destiny. When that belief dies, so will your confusion and worry.
- Multiplicity is illusory. The various types of people and things you think you see are mere modulations of the transient nature of your own experience.
- Gratitude is causeless.

- Rather than fix the problems you experience, get more interested in the nature of you, the one who experiences. If you get wrong who you are, everything you experience will be wrong too.

- Seekers are made of precisely what they seek.

- Kids who are struggling don't desire a cognitive theory, a coping method, or a magic cure. They require presence; they desire love.

- To believe is to "not know."

- If you're told to sit down and stop rocking the boat, keep rocking. If the boat were stable, if the boat were honest, if the boat were true, it couldn't be rocked in the first place.

- Not what you see on the news, not what a study depicts, not what anyone (including me) says—listen to and follow your own experience. Nothing else will ever reveal the truth.

- Who are you? The dreamer or the character within the dream? Either way, you're not in command. The dream unfolds as it will. So let go and truly live.

- A paradox of teaching *non-duality* is that we must use words, and words are designed to clarify the appearance of *duality*. This is why non-duality can seem confusing. Contradictions come with the territory.

- Has the belief, theory, or strategy that you're offering as a remedy for suffering remedied your own suffering? Then why are you offering it to others?

- Take everything to be the opposite of the way it appears. Life will be effortless.

- So-called "negative feelings" are simply sensations taken personally. This is why addressing feelings is ineffective. They're neutral. The personalization and depersonalization of any sensation or experience is where suffering begins and ends.

- It's not an error to sense that "I am a body-mind." It's an error to believe that "I am a body-mind."

- We must constantly ask ourselves whether the basis from which we're living has been ingrained in us or experienced by us. For if it has been ingrained, it is not true. And living from mistruth, living a life based on belief, is the root of perpetual confusion, suffering, and conflict.

- The point of science, a field of study that evolves, is not to put our trust in science. The point of science is to discover what does not evolve and put our trust in that.

- Competition does not = winning at the expense of others. Competition = cooperation, love, or the absence of others.

- Even if the belief in duality has vanished, the illusion forever remains.
- When we observe ignorant or arrogant behavior, it's essential to remember that what we see isn't occurring "out there." We are Consciousness; we are always observing the inner workings of ourselves.
- Opinions are harmless—except the opinion that my opinion is better, more righteous, or higher-minded than yours.
- Insecurity is an intuitive alert, a reminder that you're connecting your well-being to the relationships, rewards, and statuses of the material world. Insecurity need not be fixed. It means you're working perfectly well.
- There's no finding success. Success is an illusory destination touted by an illusory ego to keep you distracted from Source.
- All things are made of Consciousness. Consciousness, however, is not made of these things.
- Don't show me the statistics, the words of experts, or that which has been accepted as true. Deep down in your heart, what makes sense to you? I'll listen to you. I care about you.
- Beliefs support beliefs. Place the truth—"I am not a separate self"—on your house of beliefs and it crumbles to the foundation in an instant.

- Seeking a cure for your bad habits? Wait. Every bad habit was once one of those.
- You're not a sinner, a miniscule and deficient speck within the whole, or an instrument of something greater. Stop believing what you've been taught. There's no evidence for any of it. Start examining for yourself what is true.
- Only the ego claims that "everything happens for a reason." The Self has no need to talk itself through experience. It does not mask or manage feelings. It will not attempt to cope.
- The materialistic lie we've been living will implode. That's what all lies do. The question is whether it implodes and the human race persists, or, if we don't wake up, the human race implodes too. Let's wake up.
- Do you want to discover who you are? Wonderful. Simply hold still. There's no step from you to you.
- Every young person confronts a tipping point where inner knowing starts to conflict with what society says is true. This moment is riddled with confusion and insecurity that will persist to the extent that he or she tips away from the Self and toward the do's and don'ts of others.
- Pain belongs to the universe. Offer it back. It will be readily received.

- It's crucial that we come to grips with and investigate our tendency to become indoctrinated and then to defend both the contents of our indoctrination and those who do the indoctrinating.
- Nothing is less spiritual than blindly falling in line.
- You know that pause right after you're asked and before you answer the question, "What things make you happy?" That pause *is* the answer.
- Any circumstance + the belief that the circumstance appears separate from you = the illusion of a problem.
- Direct experience is not what you see, hear, or sense. Direct experience is seeing, hearing, and sensing absent of conditioning (absent of what you've been taught). Your direct experience is your most valuable resource.
- Health is found not by building defenses, but by breaking down toxicity. Wisdom is found not by adding information, but by breaking down beliefs.
- Living harmoniously in a world of diversity hinges on knowing that there's no such thing.
- For peace, we must no longer accept that we're limited, lacking, and in need of protection. We must no longer resist or construct walls of defense. Despite any fear that might be present, we must live and love like never before.

- One secret to goal scoring is allowing the puck or ball to come to you. One secret to life is the knowing of your own Being. The true Self doesn't seek. All things seek it.

- While, at first, it seems to require effort, self-inquiry is actually the cessation of all efforts. The relaxation of tension. The fluid folding of mind into heart. We begin by exploring. Soon we surrender.

- If you must be convinced to trust—don't.

- There's no busy mind; there's only one thought at a time. There's no busy day; there's only one experience at a time. There's no busy life; there's only *here*, only *now*.

- Love is the absence of the other.
  Purpose is the absence of the goal.
  Beauty is the absence of the object.
  Intimacy is the absence of desire.

- Be true to *you*.

ACKNOWLEDGMENTS

Many years ago, a young seeker, aspiring teacher, coach, and author (me) thanked a well-known teacher, coach, and author named Richard Carlson for giving me so much of his time. Richard replied, "Garret, there's no time, there's only love."

Writing this book vividly revealed this truth. The manuscript seemed to appear in an instant, and my love for those I'm about to mention is immeasurable.

Joel Drazner, my editor, colleague, and buddy. You are astute and attentive. Your heart fills the pages of *True Self*. To Ruth Goodman, your keen eye brought clarity and structure to the process both early on and late. Rodrigo Corral is a master of design who honored me with this book's cover and graced me with his presence. Justin Branch, Tyler LeBleu, Erin Brown, Killian Piraro, Kimberly Lance, and the team at Greenleaf were once again a dream to work with. Thank you for your continued integrity, efficiency, and guidance.

To my sister, Karen LeFurgy, along with my friends Ali Scott, Grayson Hart, Lee Adair, Joakim Hilton, Tony Arribas, Jamie Smart, Regina Mongelli, Peter Dodd, Robert Cerfolio, Jay Blumenfeld, Brian Day, Trevor Immelman, Zach Parise,

Bill Stein, and John Gallagher—community means the world to me. And you always will too.

As you may recall, I dedicated this book to my children, their future children, and all children. There's no doubt that children hold a special place in my heart. I once saw myself as a wounded young boy. This belief took its toll. As such, I've done my best to frequently remind my wonderful children, Ryan, Jackson, and Chelsea, that the true Self cannot diminish. They are forever complete. And wouldn't you know it, as adults, they're now reminding me of the same, and others as well.

Elizabeth Kramer, the love of my life since we were teenagers at the Preakness Hills pool, I understand. Living with an explorer of true nature isn't always a piece of cake. Same goes for raising our children when I've been on the road. But somehow you managed it all with perfection. You are Consciousness in motion, pure beauty and goodness, and I love you so.

Finally, and firstly, I must express my appreciation to the true Self, Consciousness, or God's infinite Being. I'm speaking to myself, but so be it. This book is a manifestation within me, made of me, known by me. Its creation was sacred. And I'm beyond grateful that my prayers were answered and I was summoned to serve.

ABOUT THE AUTHOR

Garret Kramer is the author of two previous books, *Stillpower* and *The Path of No Resistance*. For nearly three decades, he has provided consulting services for athletes, coaches, actors, and business leaders as well as conducted workshops, daylong symposiums, and retreats for teams, organizations, and schools. Having introduced the direct path of self-exploration to the high-performance community, Garret is now sharing with global audiences his unique take on the Consciousness-only model and its implications for a more harmonious world. He lives in New Jersey, USA, with his family.